Conversations with My Other Voice: Essays

Buick Audra

Published by Trimming The Shield Records
Braidwood Drive
Nashville, TN 37214
www.trimmingtheshield.com
www.buickaudra.com

ISBN: 979-8-218-06657-4

Cover design by Buick Audra
Cover and back photos by Gregg Roth

"Voice." *Merriam-Webster.com*. 2021. https://www.merriam-webster.com (1 August 2021).

For thirteen.

Contents

Foreword

There was a three-year period during which I released my first two solo albums, *Singer* and *Family Album*. In that same window of time, I left a marriage, watched my only sibling go to prison, moved from New York to Nashville, signed a record deal, and confronted my roles in my family and my own life's story. I call that time The Great Undoing. No part of my life went unchanged. I documented those events in songs, but I never released them.

Conversations with My Other Voice presents five of those songs as they were originally written and pairs them with songs I wrote in response to them, from here. I have chosen to tell those stories that I kept hidden away for so long but decided to update the outcomes and feelings in five new songs. Each original song has an answer, and they are served up in pairs—conversations. The odd-numbered songs are the originals, and the evens are their answers. These essays expand on those narratives.

This collection is intended to accompany the album. The essays, like the songs, are presented in sets of two. They should also be read in order.

Some names and details have been omitted. Some parts of the stories do not belong to me, and so they are missing. I did my best to tell what I experienced without betraying the privacy of others.

I hope you enjoy it.

Buick Audra

This will be imperfect.

Definition of *voice*

noun

1

a

sound produced by vertebrates by means of lungs, larynx, or syrinx

especially **:** sound so produced by human beings

b

(1)

musical sound produced by the vocal folds and resonated by the cavities of head and throat

(2)

the power or ability to produce musical tones

(3)

SINGER

(4)

one of the melodic parts in a vocal or instrumental composition

(5)

condition of the vocal organs with respect to production of musical tones

(6)

the use of the voice (as in singing or acting)

c

expiration of air with the vocal cords drawn close so as to vibrate audibly (as in uttering vowels and consonant sounds as \v\ or \z\)

d

the faculty of utterance

The Melody

I once heard a music producer talk about the human voice. He had a theory that the people with the most powerful and unique singing voices had likely needed to advocate for themselves in childhood. Whether they had been born into a large family, abused, or just not heard by the adults for whatever reason: they'd had to speak up. He believed there was a connection between the two.

I do, too.

* * *

I have a big show tomorrow. I'm opening for Sara Watkins at the Franklin Theater with my whole band. I should be practicing the set, but now I hear this other melody and set of phrases that I need to follow down the rabbit hole. Songs come when they come; I've learned to listen when they do.

It's about him again. One last song to try to capture the story. It's not a love song, thank god, but it's not a hate song either. Not sure what it is yet, but it'll tell me if it wants to. Songs don't tend to show themselves unless they want to be heard.

And what exactly is the story? I know that I don't like to tell it because it makes no sense. In the past, I would try to make it about our friendship, if you can even call it that. But when I think about him now, I just think about the music. It was always my music, but I let him get tangled up in it—and for my money, that's the real narrative. Love often gets a better billing, but music is more tangible, and often, more lasting. It exists after the fact if you had the wherewithal to press "record" along the way. And I did.

So, there's a record.

* * *

We met when we were thirteen. The only truly interesting part about our meeting is that it might never have happened if my mother hadn't beat me up and put me on a plane to go live with my brother's father the week before.

One moment, I was living my thirteen-year-old life in a suburb of Boston, and the next, I was back in Miami living on fifteen acres of agricultural land in the veritable middle of nowhere with a man who was not my father. It was a hard left turn if ever there was one. I thought I'd be there for a week at most.

I was there for two and a half years.

Because my mother kicked me out in the middle of my eighth-grade year, I was again the New Kid, a role I had played many times before. I had changed schools nearly every year up to that point, but this was a mid-year shift, even more awkward. The state of not belonging anywhere or to anything might have opened me up to accepting attention from anyone. I don't mean to call him "anyone."

Well, maybe I do.

I don't know if you've ever been in the eighth grade before, but the very threshold of the thing is unsteady. When I see thirteen-year-olds now, I have to stop myself from telling them to step lightly, to be aware of what they attach themselves to—and to whom. Because it seems to me that even if you haven't just been thrown out by someone you're supposed to be able to trust, it's hard enough.

My mother sent me to Miami without any of my belongings, too. I had none of my own clothing. My first few weeks at the new school involved wearing my brother's father's XL t-shirts with things like leaping sea bass and Harley Davidson dealership logos on them. I was the New Kid *plus*. When you added that my name was Buick in a world of Heathers, Melissas, and Jennifers, I wasn't in a position to be choosy. I would sit at any lunch table with an open seat. Or pal up to any guy who shot me the occasional apathetic glance in History class. Apathetic glances are better than no glances at all, right?

Back when we still knew each other and I was a full-time fantasist, I thought of us as first loves. It was an easy anchor in an otherwise completely out-to-sea tale. Maybe we were, maybe we weren't, but the love chapter was merely a short intro to a much longer story—and throughout that story, I loved him too much.

Like all great love stories, it started with folded notes passed in hallways by peers. He wrote in shaky cursive; I wrote in loopy letters with stylized serifs. Middle school is nothing if not an opportunity to try out who you might someday be, and handwriting is part of that experiment. We quickly graduated to making out with gum in our mouths and sharing song lyrics by other people as proof of our undying, angst-ridden adoration for one another. We even shared clothing.

All told, we hung out as boyfriend and girlfriend for about a year, during which we lived in totally different worlds. His was populated by his two parents who were still married, two older sisters, and the neighborhood kids he'd known for years. He lived a ten-minute walk from our school. I lived a thirty-minute drive from the school with an assortment of people that changed all the time. I primarily lived with my brother's father, a man who acted as a father figure to me but had never been married to our mother. Months after I was sent to live with him, he entered into a serious relationship with a woman who would soon move in with her daughter, who was the same age as my brother. In addition, my brother's grandfather and his second wife lived in a house that had been built for them in the front yard. Because I lived so far from everyone I knew at school, and my brother still lived in Boston with our mother, I was on my own in this space. It was a lot to be alone with. I clung to my budding relationship as the welcome escape it was.

The thing that bonded us was not lust, emotion, or commitment; it was the shared language of music. It was ninety percent of what we spoke about. Music was the only thing either of us cared about at all, and the only job we ever wanted when we got out of there (the other ten percent of what we spoke about was how we'd get out of there). There was never a time when we weren't interacting with music, whether through imagination, conversation, practice, performance, or attendance at local shows.

Miami is a huge city. It's three times as large when you're a kid without a car. Almost all of the shows that happened near us were in Miami Beach, a separate city across a body of water. It required knowing older kids with cars or lining up an assortment of bus routes, but we were committed to the cause. A surprising number of venues allowed underage kids back then, often marking the backs of our hands with large black Xs. We attended every show we were allowed to, and that we could get a ride to. We saw all kinds of shows at the Cameo and a place called Washington Square, now long closed. I saw more than he did. I was from a lawless family with no boundaries. And Miami was a lawless city. As long as I stayed alive, I was allowed to be out. Another thing about Miami is that it's in the middle of the Atlantic Ocean, at the very bottom of

Florida, a state with which it has almost nothing in common. Its extreme geographic location means that fewer bands and artists tour through there. I tried to go see anyone who did.

Tenth grade found us attending different high schools. I was accepted to a performing arts high school in downtown Miami as a voice major. He went to the public high school near his house and started studying guitar with a private teacher. He'd already played for some time, but the lessons and stylistic explorations began that year.

During that time, there was a notable development in our lives: bands.

Seemingly overnight, every dude I knew in any capacity was in a band, whether they were a musician or not. As Steve Albini said to me when my own band was recording with him many years later, "It's not special for guys to start bands; it's almost expected of us." That was my observation as well. They were all in bands, and not one of those bands—not a single one—

had a female member. As if that wasn't enough, those of us females who knew dudes in bands were expected to attend their rehearsals.

He started a project with two older guys from my high school and a kid who was a couple of years younger. They rehearsed at someone's mom's art studio, which happened to be in a warehouse. I'm sorry to report that I was at more than a few of those rehearsals. I don't remember the band being any good, and I don't remember them ever performing an actual show. But they believed in themselves, as boys are often given permission to do.

Across town, I was studying classical voice. Part of me loved learning about different ways to use and project my voice—and how to properly breathe—but I also knew I likely wouldn't go into classical music. I wanted to write songs and sing them. My school didn't focus on that kind of vocal performance; there was a distinct emphasis on performing the work of others, whatever the genre.

I knew that I belonged in a band, too. I'd known since I was a child. But there was already a silent declaration between us that *he* was the one who would do that, and I would . . . what? Sing in the shower? Enjoy music from the audience? It was unclear. Even as kids, the message was: guys create, girls watch.

I disagreed then and I disagree now.

* * *

People who have always fit in like to assure you that you only *feel* like you don't, that it's all in your mind. Let me disabuse you of this notion. Some people are living with things that exist way outside of high school hallway dramas and difficult teen feelings. Pretending otherwise is unkind. It's also dishonest.

By the time we broke up in February of our sophomore year, I had more going on at home than I did at school. My mother had moved herself and my brother back down to Miami, into a townhouse on the other side of the city from where I'd been living. I was expected to split my time between the two households. There was a third household, but I had never been fully welcome there, and it was starting to look like I'd never visit again. It was the home of my biological father and his partner. Her two kids also lived there most of the time but spent weekends with their father who lived nearby. I'd gone to middle school with the eldest of the two kids, the son. It can't be overstated how strange it is to be in the school band with someone who lives with your father when you yourself never have. He and my mother had split when I was an infant and he'd been peripheral for most of my life up to that point. He'd taken me to see his mother in Clearwater right after Christmas in my sophomore year but hadn't called or returned my calls since. The last thing he said to me in my mother's driveway when he dropped me off was, "I'll call you next week."

After the breakup, I still saw my ex all the time. Our social group was mostly shared, and even though we went to different high schools, we crossed paths more than was helpful. He immediately got involved with someone else and I jumped around from one three-week boyfriend to the next. The only through-line among them was Drakkar Noir cologne and Nag Champa incense. High school might be more ridiculous than middle school.

I did my best to feel the way he looked: unfazed. It was as though we'd never known each other intimately at all; any expression that challenged that was untidy and unwelcome. I tiptoed away from our social circle—away from teendom altogether.

Meanwhile, my life between the two homes was one of staying in my room and listening to music. At my brother's father's home, I had been asked not to sing in the house because it made my now stepsister insecure about her own voice. I was a voice major. I started to spend more time at my mother's place. That house was tiny and full, so singing became an in-school-only activity. I was performing in college operas by then, as a chorus member or child character. I loved it. In one production I played a young boy, and my chest was bound, forcing my breathing to truly come from my diaphragm. It was the most uncomfortable but effective way to learn to breathe from the bottom, not the top. I liked performing with the college students. It provided a sense of purpose even though I knew I wanted to write music, not perform the work of others. It was still an education and a welcome distraction. At home, I was studying the great songwriters and singers, listening to what they did and how.

Toward the end of the year, I attended two different senior proms with older platonic friends of mine. The day after the second prom, I walked into my mother's bedroom and said something that had been living in my mouth for as long as I'd had memories. An encounter the night before had triggered a nervous system response in my body and I knew it was time. I told her about the sexual abuse I'd endured at the hands of my brother's grandfather, the old man who lived on the property where I had just spent the last two years. He'd been my babysitter from a young age and was unfit to be around children, something I'm certain was known by the adults before I was born. I'd been avoiding him and his wife the whole time I'd been back in town.

The news ripped through the branches of my family like a fire. It quickly morphed from a truth to a story I was telling to be hurtful, and the following month of my life was consumed with navigating other peoples' experiences with it. My mother believed me but took full custody of the injury and wore it as her own. My brother's father and the surrounding family claimed not to believe me and took to shaming me for saying such a thing—as if sixteen-year-old kids have nothing better to do with their time. You think that when you open your mouth and speak, you will be believed. At sixteen, I learned the opposite. I was told I needed to be the bigger person, I was separated from my only sibling so as to not influence him, and I was sent a box of all the gifts, cards, and letters I'd ever given to the grandfather figure and his wife. It came with a letter from her calling me a lying whore.

And yet, every time I showed up to school, the teen world continued to turn. Kids were still playing shaky renditions of "Nothing Else Matters" on hundred-dollar guitars during lunch under the shade of Banyan trees. Cheerleaders were still cheering. My ex and his new love were still nauseating, now in matching dark blue ten-hole Doc Martens boots. I felt like I was performing myself as a Regular Kid. No script.

The expectation to keep going when you have nowhere to go can be baffling.

Somewhere across town, my biological father was unbothered and unaware. If he knows any of this happened, I couldn't tell you. I did not hear from him again.

* * *

My mother decided to move the three of us back up to Boston that summer. She planned to go in August, but I couldn't wait that long. I left when school let out and spent the summer with my best friend Jared at his dad's house in Belmont, Massachusetts. I listened to

Soundgarden and dreamed about starting a band. I slept on a mattress on the living room floor but felt more welcome than I had in years. I felt wanted, even. It was new.

* * *

It wouldn't be opera. It wouldn't be concert choir or jazz ensemble. I had tried on all of those and worn them like costumes that fit but would eventually have to be taken off. Somehow, I would figure out how to make music in a way that felt like my natural skin, my own self—and that didn't rely on anyone else. It would involve instruments and experimentation. I could handle that.

Once I moved, communication with my ex fell away. We no longer had cause to run into each other and trade nonsense niceties. I assumed he would ride off into the sunset with the infinitely less complicated person he'd found, and she'd be suitably impressed by that one Crowded House guitar part he knew how to play. Good. Let her sit in warehouses with no air circulating while his bands practiced their five whole songs; let her pretend to be interested.

I was starting fresh. I would write songs and play them and have my own band practices that no women would be expected to attend. I could change the whole thing if I wanted.

After all, I was sixteen years old. Almost free.

Pocket-Sized Friend

We were almost put on the same bill together here in Nashville a few months ago. The very idea of it sent my whole body into a panic response. My temperature spiked and I broke into a spontaneous sweat. I called a friend who knew a little about the history; it was a miscalculation on my part. After telling me that I was overreacting, he announced that he didn't "have things like this," meaning estrangements.

I've since come to understand that the people who say things like that are the ones other people choose to be estranged from, not the other way around. They're also the same people who don't think anyone should have feelings. My mistake. Again.

* * *

The boundary had been like an amputation. I had tried other times and failed. A few years would pass, and we would wander back into each other's life; the whole cycle would repeat itself like we'd never learned anything the previous times. But I was starting to have wounds to show for those other laps around the route. I wasn't doing so well. In the same way that you might not notice you've had back pain for ten years before a doctor asks you about it directly, I was just living with it. I thought it was normal.

It wasn't until he'd been out of my life for several years that I started to be able to see the true extent of the damage. I thought I couldn't hear pitch correctly; I wouldn't track vocals with an engineer; I nearly gave up playing guitar on my recordings, and I believed I was the weak link in all of my relationships, musical or otherwise. I wasn't born with those ideas. They were given to me on a slow drip that I called friendship; that I protected at all costs; that I went back for time and again.

That I trusted.

Other ideas I held about myself included: emotionally unstable, an unreliable witness to my own experience, too much, too little, and in need of assistance—especially when it came to my music. Those had a little help from my family.

When I set the boundary, I didn't have language around any of that. I just knew it was time to cut it off. For the thousandth time, he'd been available and then absent. For the thousandth time, we'd made a bunch of work together followed by a freeze. For the thousandth time, it was my fault, and I couldn't navigate it anymore. I cut ties from a Penske truck somewhere in Wyoming, driving a friend and her belongings across the country. And this time, I asked him to never contact me again. I would figure out life and music on my own from there, thank you very much.

We had almost had a clean break early on, when I moved away from Miami, and he stayed behind. He would have become one name among many whose writings were scribbled on folded up notes in a shoebox, a face in a yearbook in the basement. A paper graveyard of boys you used to kiss.

That's not what happened.

We made it a few years after I moved to Boston from Miami. Fifteen hundred miles with no phone calls, no social media, and no contact between us. And then one day, I heard from him. He was coming to town to visit one of his sisters who was at Boston University. We got together on that trip, and then we were back in touch. The following year, he moved to Boston to attend Berklee. I was at MassArt. We started separate bands and co-existed in a scene that seemed big enough for both of us. I hired him to record my demos on an ADAT machine in his basement a couple of times.

There were warning signs before it—little side comments about my pitch, my ear, my understanding of music—but the first big flags came after my band 33 Slade made our first album with J. Robbins at Inner Ear in Arlington, Virginia. Suddenly he was entitled to critiques of the record, the guitar sounds, my vocal approach. He was entitled to his voiced opinion. He was entitled.

This was familiar to me. My mother spoke to me about my musicianship in this way. There was never a compliment. Not for me, anyway. The compliments were reserved for everyone around me, which in the case of this particular project was her other kid—my brother—and our friend Levi. The guys. They really had it together, she said. Me? Less so. Her precise words to me when she heard our first record were, "You guys will be great when you get a real guitar player."

I was the guitar player.

His commentary, while less biting, was of a similar style. It was always presented as fact, instead of the unsolicited opinion it was. To me, this was what family felt like. He had been like family when we were younger—when my own family had not. He was back in my life and paying attention to me, which seemed to be the goal even though I could never articulate why.

I kept making records, he kept being nearby, and eventually we sat down and collaborated. We'd written one song together when we were about twenty-one, back in Miami on Christmas break from our respective college experiences. We circled back for that one and wrote three more. We decided to record them as an EP at a studio where I'd already started 33 Slade's second album, Camp Street in Cambridge. I enlisted the help of a friend who worked out of Camp Street at the time, and with whom I was working on the other project. His name was Matt Squire, and he joined us for a day as the engineer; he ended up playing drums on one song, too. It was a light day of collaboration and tracking that left me feeling like the dynamic was one I could return to.

A few months later, 33 Slade did a tour opening for a popular songwriter and his band. Our founding bass player had moved to Seattle, so I asked my now old Miami friend to fill in. He was primarily a guitarist, but he prided himself on being multi-instrumental. He'd known my brother and me for many years at that point. We thought it would be fine for a week.

The tour started out well enough. We rented a van, had our act as together as it was ever going to be, and headed out. But the behavior started shortly after. We'd get off stage, and he would immediately tell me what I had done wrong. It was swift and cutting. It was sometimes my guitar playing, but it was always my voice. My voice was failing me every night because, he explained, my ears were hearing things incorrectly. My pitch was all over the place, he claimed. It was the strangest thing. I felt like I could hear fine, and my voice sounded the way it always did. Had I never been able to hear correctly?

* * *

When I was five or six years old, a man who was close friends with my brother's father tried to push me out of a moving car when we were all in Martha's Vineyard. It happened on a night when two of my aunt figures took me out to a bar with them, lost their keys, and then called one of their partners to come pick us up. Substances were

involved and the collective judgement of the adults was skewed. The women put me in the front seat with the man, and as he drove us back to the rental house, he opened my door and started to push me out. It was his response to the women and their fighting. It was his punishment. I can still see the pavement whipping by between the door and the body of the car.

When I told my brother's father about it, he responded by saying it never happened, that I had misremembered. I maintained my account of the story throughout the rest of my childhood, adolescence, and eventual adulthood, and he maintained that it had not happened.

* * *

I was familiar with being told that my experience of a thing was incorrect. I found it frightening. To think that we might not be seeing life through a clear lens is disorienting, at minimum.

My brother and I didn't know how to deal with it. He spoke up, I spoke up, we told our interim third member to knock it off. But it went on. The Brooklyn show was the most extreme. We played a sold-out show, and the actual minute we left the stage, he started in on me. That time I had a physical reaction—one that has recurred. To this day, whenever I feel like I've made a mistake on stage, my system goes into a sensory overdrive that I have to live through and wait out. I sweat, I shake, and my hands become less able to do their job. When I'm playing guitar and this happens, it can interrupt a song.

We had one night at home in Boston before the last show of the tour, which was to be in Buffalo. I chose to drop off the tour and not play the final show. I couldn't imagine getting on stage with that dynamic one more time. I didn't believe I could play or sing.

And that was it. I let my own opportunity go. The one I'd earned with my own music. I allowed someone to be bigger than me in my own story, and in my own band for which I wrote all the music. I was more focused on being ashamed of myself than I was on his trespassing.

That time, we didn't speak for two years.

* * *

I blame chance and circumstance for the next encounter. Somehow, even though I was living in Brooklyn and he was living in San Diego, we ran into each other in Coconut Grove in Miami around Christmas, more than two-and-a-half years after the tour debacle. I was with my mother, brother, and then-husband. He was with his longtime friend-turned-business partner. They had recently opened a recording studio out West. I was looking to start work on my first full-length solo album, one that I could really lean into producing. I'd made one solo electric EP when I first moved to New York the year before, but I wanted to go big this time; have a full band and then some. I would call it *Singer*.

Here was another opportunity to leave this person in the paper graveyard of a journal, but no.

Something about the friendliness of the two groups encountering one another allowed me to ignore my own past story and agree to work with him on the record at their new studio. Let me be honest: it was my idea. I thought I'd finally be able to prove my musical mettle. To him, to me, and probably on some level, to my family. I can blame chance for the encounter, but the next bit was all me. The road to bad ideas is paved with even worse self-beliefs, tell you what.

We started work on the album two months later. I flew out from Brooklyn and had my former 33 Slade bandmates join me there for the first sessions. We started out alright. We did. Boey, Levi, and I were used to working together, and we'd all known him for varying lengths of time. Boey had decided to let the bad behavior of the tour live in the past tense; he was likely following my lead. We were all showing up as our adult selves, ready to render this thing I heard in my head. I had already done some pre-production with everyone, and really, he was supposed to be engineering, period. Harmless. In that first few days of making the record, I was reminded of how much I loved recording. I was thrilled to be at it again.

I flew back to San Diego several times over the following fifteen months to make the album. Some of it was wonderful, exciting, and funny. We laughed a lot. We laughed ourselves right out of being able to function. We worked long, ridiculous days in an attempt to maximize on my time out there. I could only afford to go every few months, and even then, I was staying with him instead of at a hotel or somewhere more private. We were on top of each other in and out of the studio. There was a familiar immediacy to our time together.

Other times, it came apart. And when it did, injuries were sustained.

The mythology he had started building years earlier around my ability to hear pitch was back. I'd sing a song multiple times and listen back on the monitors, and it would sound fine. Then we'd listen in the car, and the vocal would be out in the slightest of ways, but throughout the entire track. It was clear that I was hearing the track in a weird way when I was singing. And instead of investigating his own space or the way we were tracking or listening back, the fault landed on me. I took the blame right into my veins. I wore that belief like a tattoo. "I can't hear pitch" was a new truth to carry right alongside "I'm too sensitive" and "I don't fit in anywhere." What's one more when you already have a collection going?

I did push back here and there. It was one thing to be told that I couldn't hear pitch, but I had a harder time accepting the direction not to push as hard as I wanted to when I sang. One song in particular required more power than the others because of where it sat in my range. It was a song called "Brilliant Mistakes." Not only was it high in my voice, but I'd written it about my brother's arrest earlier that year. At the time of its recording, we were waiting to hear how long he'd spend in prison. It was a season of heightened emotions and the song reflected that. The idea that I should try to sing it with less power was untenable to me. I asked him to leave me alone in the studio so that I could record the vocals myself, without his feedback. He reluctantly obliged. He napped in the office while I sang. To my ears, it's the best performed vocal on the album. I think you can tell I wasn't afraid of failing anyone else.

When we finally wrapped the album and he was set to start mixing it, the question of who would master it arose. I'd only made rock records up to that point, so I hadn't yet worked with mastering engineers who did country and americana records. I got out all the records I had ever loved by singer-songwriters and looked at the liner notes. One name appeared more than anyone else's: Doug Sax.

I looked him up.

It turned out that Doug Sax did still master records, up in Ojai. I booked a date with him and chose to attend the session. I'd never been to a mastering session before and was curious about how it worked. My mastering date was in May of that year. I would be in San Diego for the mixing beforehand, and then I would drive up to Sax's studio for the mastering session. The engineer decided to come along and see "what someone who charges that much really does." Not an ideal attitude, but I let him join.

The Mastering Lab was one of the most efficient studios I've ever entered. The minute we walked in, our hard drive was gently taken from us, plugged in, and a transfer was started. Coffee was offered, introductions were given, jokes were made. It was the Wash & Brush Up Company of mastering studios.

Doug Sax was about seventy then. He had absolutely nothing to prove, having already won the Lifetime Achievement Grammy, and having worked on some of the most notable records of all time. He still had a lot to offer, though. On that day, Doug Sax changed the course of my life.

He took a shine to me right away. He liked my songs, and he said so. He hit and shook an air tambourine every time he heard something he liked, a delightful and funny experience each time. He listened with his eyes closed, occasionally turning around to adjust knobs on his unmarked equipment that he had designed and built. When he had notes or questions, he addressed them right to me, never to my engineer. He complimented me and occasionally criticized the work of the engineer, pointing out mix problems or things he would have approached differently. At one point, he suggested the engineer start reading magazines related to recording and mixing—a moment that mortified the engineer. I was in awe.

I don't know exactly what Doug saw in our dynamic, but he didn't like it. It was the first time in our lives that anyone had looked at us and seen the imbalance. Up to that point, I had been told I was lucky to have the engineer. I was lucky when we were kids, lucky when we were briefly bandmates, lucky he was my friend, and lucky he was my collaborator. My family tended to put me below whoever stood next to me, and for many years, in many different scenarios, it had been him. Doug would have none of it.

Every now and then, Doug would open his eyes and peer over at me. It was as though he was trying to tell me something he didn't want to say aloud. Instead, he said, "You remind me of Jackson Browne. He's like you. He comes to the sessions; he takes his records seriously." I thanked him and nodded. Browne's records were among the many I'd seen Doug's name on. Toward the end of the session, Doug turned to my engineer and said, "Stick with her. You might learn something." No smile, no air tambourine. Just the words. He said them like he meant them.

As I finalized things with his office manager and assistants, Doug told me he was going to call his friend in Nashville, a recording engineer who doubled as an A&R rep for a label. He told me to go to Nashville, to meet this guy and other people in the community. What he didn't say out loud was, *Get away from this other guy. It's of no benefit to you to keep him around.* But I heard it.

If the car wheels were on the road during the drive back to San Diego, I couldn't feel them. I was flying.

The engineer and I made two more records together. Well, one and part of another. The sessions for my second LP, *Family Album*, began before I released *Singer*. He was involved from the outset, though my vision for that record was entirely different. I wanted no studio sessions, aiming instead for whole thing to be tracked in homes, starting with my brother's before he was incarcerated. That was why we started when we did. A clock was ticking, and I wanted to get my brother on there before everything changed.

I also enlisted his help for the last vocal sessions on an album I made with Joss Stone. He came in right at the end, but he was there, and he saw it. And then we never saw each other again. The bad outweighed the good and I couldn't change the ratio. Sometimes you can't. I had spent a lot of my life trying, and also trying to make myself the size and shape he had wanted me to be, to no avail. I still apologize to myself for it on a regular basis.

* * *

More than a year after the last sessions for *Family Album*, I went back to Ojai to master it with Doug Sax. I was alone this time. After we all settled in for the session, Doug looked over at me and said, "Where's the other one?" I looked back and said, "Gone. For good." He nodded and said, "Good. I thought so."

And then he mastered my record. The music had been mine all along, and Doug had known it. He had been waiting for me to figure it out.

I had.

Definition of *voice*

noun

2

a sound resembling or suggesting vocal utterance

Afraid of Flying

The woman seated next to me was making polite small talk about why we were both traveling. We were on an overnight flight from New York to England. She told me she was returning home from a trip to the States. She was a high-ranking member of the Quaker Church who had been traveling for a conference. I told her I was traveling to England to work on a promising new business venture with a woman I'd known a short while.

"Do you have a good conflict resolution practice in place together?" she asked.

"No, but we get along really well," I replied.

Famous last words.

* * *

The text read: "Congratulations. You just became a Grammy winner."

It was sent by a friend of mine who's at the Grammys tonight. He knew before I did because he's in attendance through all of the categories that aren't televised, like gospel, roots music, and classical. He was nominated tonight, too. He's always nominated.

I'm home alone. We've had nine inches of snow fall on the ground today, which in Nashville, is called a blizzard. I ordered Chinese food from four blocks away and it took over an hour to get here. Still, I'm grateful for it. I've been in my pajamas pacing around the house, occasionally calling people I shouldn't, to tell them news that they don't know how to respond to. I wish someone else was here. Not her, but someone.

We *won*. I *knew* we would, but also couldn't believe it at exactly the same time. Best Traditional Gospel Album, and we were the eleventh track, the last track. I liked that we were last. It felt like we punctuated the project. It had sure as hell had punctuated my life. I never tell anyone the story. People want to believe that flying back and forth to England to make music with someone they've heard of is enchanting, exciting. They don't want to hear about your panic attacks; or how she decided the recording sessions would happen overnight and you never quite adjusted; or that you were lonely all the time; or how she laughed at you. Let's face it: you don't even want to hear that last one. So, you smile and nod when people say you're lucky, and you deal with it on your own.

And now there's a Grammy. She hasn't called and I won't call either. No one but the executive producer attends the awards when a compilation is nominated, so all of us artists are scattered, getting texts and calls from people who are there in person, or who are updating the website to see who's won what.

I made the mistake of telling my parents. My mother went right to making sure I don't make my brother feel too badly about it, because he's still in prison. My brother's father was silent for a long time and then said, "Well. It's a start."

But it's not a start. It's an end.

* * *

I had never heard her music when we first met. I knew she went barefoot on stage and that she was something of a modern flower child. I also didn't care. I'd been called in by her stylist to design and make some items for her, and that I could do. I worked with a lot of people whose work I didn't know. My job was to make them look great and feel confident in whatever I designed and built. The first couple of things I made for her were received well, so I saw her every few months after that when she was in the States.

She didn't know I was also a musician. In the world of celebrity fashion, I never mentioned my own music, though it was what I spent all my time, money, and energy doing. I learned early on that most people only see the basest thing about you, and they see it forever. To some people, I will always be a tailor and designer. I could win Album of the Year and they'd be like, "Not her, she sews."

You never told the celebrities about your other pursuits for fear that you'd come off as someone trying to break ranks in this absolutely ranked world. Your own art was something that happened off the clock and behind the scenes.

The years that I designed for her overlapped with the time I spent making and releasing my first full-length solo album, *Singer*. I named it that as a declaration of what I am, of how I see myself. We might not be able to change how we are seen by others, but we can certainly update how we see ourselves. I was aiming to do exactly that.

I lived in Brooklyn at the time but was making *Singer* in San Diego with a childhood friend-turned-collaborator who owned a studio out there. Additional recording was done in New York and Boston. The project took more than a year to make, in fits and starts, but I worked on it as I could afford to. Would it have been cheaper to make it locally instead of travelling? Sure. It would have saved me a lot more than money, too, but I wasn't in the business of sparing myself anything back then.

The night before I got *Singer* mastered, I took my collaborator to see Joss play at a casino in San Diego. She and I had worked together for a couple of years by then and were friendly. He and I were put on the guest list by her people, and we visited with her backstage after the show. Perhaps because we were in a different setting, perhaps because I was giddy with new album confidence, I gave her a copy of the unmastered album. It remains the only I time I've done anything of the sort.

Earlier that day, my co-producer and I had gotten matching tattoos on our ribs. Gramophones. The symbol of the Grammys. We did it to be funny, but also maybe to etch it into existence, into our flesh. We had shared a dream for a life of music since we were thirteen. We thought, *why not? What's a little real estate on one's ribcage when we're making our intentions known?*

It was a whirlwind thirty-six hours that changed the way I saw all kinds of things, including myself. Doug Sax had blessed *Singer*—and by extension, me—and I had more belief in myself than was typical. I flew home from California with a finished album and my head held high. I forgot about giving her the record.

Months later, after a fitting in Manhattan, Joss invited me to dinner with her stylist and two other people. I accepted, assuming we'd talk shop about her upcoming appearances, some of which I had designed garments for. She surprised me by singing at the top of her lungs in a full restaurant. It was hard to say which was more surprising, the singing or the fact that she was singing my song, "Happy Loser," from my still unreleased album. She had listened to it.

She said, "I might record that song. Or maybe we should record it!" By the end of dinner, she was talking about us making an album of duets together. I didn't believe a word of it; people said wild things all the time in the entertainment industries. They rarely materialized. It seemed believable to me that this woman who was comfortable singing loudly at tables might also be the type to get overly enthusiastic about ideas that would never take shape.

Yes and no.

By the following month, not only we were going to make an album together, but we were also going to have a clothing line. It all piled up quickly. I was saying yes to everything without thinking about it. It was intoxicating to have someone want to work with me, to want to join forces. She was quick to excitement, she breezed past unpleasantness, and mostly, she made things seem easy. I loved that about her. I didn't know much about ease. I was ready to learn.

The first flight was to Los Angeles. I met her out there to show her my sketches for our all-of-a-sudden clothing line I had designed in a pinch. While I was there, I swatched fabrics to gather ideas for color, texture, and weight. We talked about the album, too. She had airy musings about making it in a single week, the way one might throw together a backyard party. My experience with albums had been the opposite. They were Herculean efforts that took time, labor, and money. Maybe we'd land on something in the middle. Maybe that would be true of the music styles, too. Maybe lots of things.

* * *

I moved to Nashville shortly thereafter and began flying back and forth between there and England every few months. She and I started writing the record on my first trip over there. She didn't play an instrument, so the chord progressions and structures were left to me. We wrote the lyrics and vocal melodies together. Her writing style was such that she would start singing something and I'd try to grab it out of thin air and negotiate it into a song form, either existing or new. We recorded all our writing sessions so that the song ideas would be captured along with any other promising tidbits we might circle back for.

She lived in rural England, the kind of place that still looked almost exactly like *The Princess Bride*. The homes were set back in the green countryside. The residential neighborhood roads were called lanes, single-car-width passages between tall hedges that scraped against the cars as they whipped through. People honked as they approached turns, to warn any oncoming vehicles that they were there. Cars crashed often and no one seemed to mind. It was as scenic as it was isolating. Her family and close friends lived all around her, and many of them also worked for her. I was in her world day and night, and I didn't have a vehicle. Even if I had, with the driving being the stuff of nightmares and/or Edgar Wright films, I could never have pulled it off. I was reliant on others to get around, to eat, and to live. Not ideal.

On my first two trips, I stayed at her place, or at inn above a local pub. I had doors that closed for a few hours each day. That was more important than I understood at the time. When I was on my own at night, I would do my best to sort through whatever had been created or discussed that day, to make notes and connections between conversations and songs. I would also write songs on my own. Writing music had become how I journaled, how I processed my experiences. I took a couple of those compositions to her, and she pushed to add them to the pile of songs we would perform together. She wrote a few lines for each of them, so she would have some creative ownership of the work.

I did like singing with her. For as different as our voices and styles were on our own, we sounded quite natural together. On the recordings of the writing sessions, as soon as we start singing, it becomes difficult to identify who's who. I hadn't had that in years, singing with a woman. I'd sung plenty with my brother and other guys, but not with a woman. The first couple of songs we wrote were pretty good, too. They landed somewhere between my singer-songwriter, americana leanings and her neo-soul stylings. I was surprised by how well it worked. And I had never written so rapidly. We would sometimes write two or three songs in a day when I was there.

It was invigorating to be living a life centered around making music. I had always had to do something else to make money—sometimes several things at once—just to be able to make my music. She had never lived that life. She had become famous in her teens. So, when I was on her turf, I lived like that, too.

But my life wasn't like that. I was struggling.

As months passed and the project grew, I was broke, sleeping in her mother and stepfather's small study on a chaise lounge, and starting to experience symptoms of post-traumatic stress disorder. I would lie awake for hours, my thoughts dark and devoid of hope. I came to learn that they were panic attacks, but I'd never had them before. I didn't know how to talk about it. She and I didn't have the kind of relationship that allowed for any real intimacy—even at our friendliest points—so I did my best to act as if I was doing well. In turn, she made clear that not being able to cut it on the kind of schedule she'd had to maintain in her career, was weakness. All roads led back to her story; I was learning.

I was also learning that there is an ocean between friendly and friends.

By the time we were ready to start recording the album, I was raw but still moving ahead. We had written more than a dozen songs across several genres. Decisions about what, where, and who were thrown together, and dates were set. She invited two members of her touring band to perform with us on the album and I invited a guy I'd had a brief, ill-advised relationship with, but with whom I'd also collaborated; he was a bluegrass guitar player in Nashville. I figured I could make it through a few more weeks of living away from my actual life. I was used to her world in a way—not comfortable, but familiar.

And then it changed.

I don't know why I didn't see it coming. I wanted so badly to believe that we could do this thing, that *I* could do it. I'd thrown so much at it, given so much unpaid labor. I'd even built the samples for the entire debut collection of our clothing line. What were three more weeks?

Denial sometimes dresses up as hope.

We set up in the studio above the venue/cafe that her mother and stepfather owned. It was modest but fine for what we were trying to accomplish. We couldn't track as a band, but we'd all made enough records to be comfortable with layering our performances. She and I would act as producers. That had been the plan from the beginning. I loved producing and very much wanted to shape the assorted songs into a body of work that would make sonic and thematic sense.

Very quickly, I learned that the presence of the men changed everything. Because two of them worked for her, they were both familiar with and loyal to her. And the guy that I brought was much more concerned with her opinion of him than he was with mine or the record being any good. The fourth man working on the project was her stepfather and former live drummer whose studio we were using. I held no cards. It was no longer about the two of us and the songs we had written. It was about her—and for me, too, it was about her. I wanted to regain her attention, her approval, her friendship. But the more I wanted that, the more strained the situation became. By the second week, I was eating alone on breaks and caving in on myself.

The tracking would go well until it didn't, and then it would be about me. She started to focus on my vocals and what she didn't like about them; she spoke loudly about it in front of everyone else and had me re-sing things with an audience. That wasn't right for me. I don't benefit from that kind of setting; she didn't care.

In turn, I had some questions about who was getting to sing what—and how aggressively, but those were questions that didn't get asked as often as they might have in another context. I wasn't getting her to re-sing anything. She had been told she was a wonder all her life. I had lived at the other end of that spectrum. And there we were.

The England sessions were the first time I noted the difference between singing to tell the truth and singing to win. They're remarkably different.

I was the one to introduce the idea of a cover song. Sometimes someone else's words can help a situation. I played her my version of "Wildflowers" by Tom Petty, a song I'd leaned on heavily when my brother was first taken into custody, when I was leaving my life in Brooklyn behind. The idea of belonging somewhere you feel free had been healing for me in other areas, and I thought it might be a salve to our relationship, our project. She loved the song, which she had somehow never heard before. A day later, she brought a song to the table for us to cover as well, "This Little Light of

Mine," a song I associated with the Civil Rights movement, but which also had a home in the gospel world. I felt a little unsure about both of those affiliations, as a white atheist. But she had been open to my cover suggestion, so we did it.

The idea for "This Little Light of Mine" was a complete departure from the rest of the album, which had been built layer by layer. The approach was to do it live, with one microphone. By that point in the record, we were sleeping during the day and tracking through the night (her preference), so our version of "This Little Light of Mine" was cut at 7 AM, at the end of a session, in a stairway. All three of us guitarists played; we'd worked out the parts in advance. A local harmonica player joined us on the track, the bass player played acoustic bass, and Joss and I sang. We did two complete passes of the song. She preferred the second one, so that's what was chosen.

By the end of the England sessions, we had recorded thirteen original songs and two covers. Fifteen songs in total. We needed one more, to be written later, so that it would line up with the number of looks in our debut clothing line. We decided to call the album *Sixteen Songs* by Joss Stone and Buick Audra. She explained that her name was known and should therefore be first. She was right, but I'd never heard anyone say anything like that before. I was both in awe of the confidence and repelled by it. I didn't even know if the music was any good. I was sleep-deprived and deeply ashamed of my own existence.

I left England two days before Christmas, unable to turn my head from side to side, unsure of what had just transpired. But somewhere on a hard drive lived a recording wherein I convincingly sang, "This little light of mine, I'm gonna let it shine." And I had, sort of. I might have been worn down and separate by the end, but I was still standing; I had still done the damn thing.

Sometimes you don't end up with a friend or a cheerful story you'll tell for years. Sometimes you end up with a Grammy and a story you wait a very long time to tell anyone, even yourself. Sometimes the lesson is: you were brave, and you tried, so enjoy the tofu and broccoli while you watch the snow pile up in your front yard. You're safe now. And if anybody tells you you're lucky to have a Grammy, you tell them you earned it.

You did.

From Down Here

In my late teens, a woman in the Boston music scene asked me to do a project with her in which we both played guitar and sang. We did it for a couple of years until my other band, 33 Slade, became more primary. But when we were still in the project, the dynamic was strange. She was several years older than me and felt like she knew better what we needed to wear, play, and do. She even wanted to direct the way I looked in my everyday life.

Our friendship lasted a little bit after the project ended, but ultimately fell apart and the unkindness it bred was something I spent years unpacking. The thing that stung most was the collapse of my own feminist fantasy, the one that led me to believe that even an ending would be handled with dignity and respect for both parties. Instead, it gave way to a scorched earth kind of hell.

My mind tends to dull the edges of blades I have known.

* * *

A couple of months in my new-but-empty Nashville home did me good. I had started seeing someone during the months of traveling back and forth to England; the time at home allowed me to spend some time with him, and also with myself. Nashville didn't necessarily feel like home to me yet, but neither did anywhere else. It would do for the time being. I spent my days trying to make enough money to live, write songs, chip away at a record I was making with people I considered family, and recover. The England sessions were behind me, and I could move forward with whatever lay ahead.

When I heard from Joss again, the new message was that my vocals on the record weren't good enough. Hers were fine; mine needed work. At first, that made sense to me. England had been such a drag, it stood to reason that I might not have done my best work. I agreed to re-approach them. I offered an option: instead of flying back to England, I could find a studio in the States and re-record my parts there. I'd then send them back to her and she'd decide if they were good enough to be released. I, believing in more than one fairytale at a time, called an engineer with whom I had a dodgy but long relationship. He had a studio in San Diego. I'd already made an entire record there, and he would be honest with me about my vocals. That much, I could guarantee.

It had only been two months since I'd left England and I was already willing to return to the project, to her. Like a marriage that was on its last legs, I resented the amount of time, effort, and emotional labor I'd already invested, and was convinced I could see it through to a better ending. She, like my mother, was the type to breeze past all horrors of the past and cheerfully move on. I had already logged many years of training in how to conform to that attitude, so I kept going. As it turns out, you can get used to anything.

I flew to San Diego as directed and waited for her to send the files of the songs. It didn't exactly line up. The engineer and I had a good amount of downtime, during which we demoed one of my solo songs because we had nothing else to do. Finally, we got some session files from her and got to work. Some of them, though, were missing. In two months, she'd already lost some of the music we'd made together, including the first song we'd ever written, "Songs About Boys." It had been my favorite song from our fifteen-song catalog. She was already past it, and I was expected to be, as well. The name of the game with her was recalibrate, retool, and require nothing. I tried. We never did get the full number of files for the songs she wanted me to re-sing, so I sang what I could and flew home to Nashville.

And then, I signed to her record label. The process had been in motion for several months. She had started the label to sign me, a gesture I'd initially taken as a compliment. I had never had a record deal before. At first, the label was going to be an imprint of the major label she was affiliated with, but her relationship with that label was collapsing. She ended up starting her label as a freestanding independent with some input from high-profile industry figures. She gave the label a name that was a riff on her stage name, drew up some logo that looked like an illustration in the margin of a high schooler's notebook, and blazed ahead. I signed my end of things in the office of my entertainment lawyer on Music Row in Nashville. I signed in purple ink. We took photos that I have never looked at again, but which felt momentous at the time.

Signing felt like a new chance. She still wanted to work with me, and I was willing to see the whole thing through. The general idea of what we were trying to do was good, I thought. I loved the idea of being in business with another woman in the music world. Our industry was dominated by cis men at every level. Here, we had this opportunity to make something new, something cool, something female. Who cared if there was rainstick and no thematic through-line to speak of? These were minor details in the bigger picture of the feminist empire we were building.

Friends, a feminist empire requires that there be feminism in the first place. Write it down.

Right after my signing, a gospel compilation was released by EMI, her label at the time. Our 7 AM rendition of "This Little Light of Mine" was the last track on the record. We were in the company of Al Green, Mavis Staples, Michael McDonald, and all kinds of other legendary folks. I bought a physical copy of it in the store. It was wild to see my name on there. As I held it in my hands, I knew it would be nominated for a Grammy. Some things are simply known, not necessarily wanted.

Shortly after that, I was told that my vocals on the album still weren't good enough. The San Diego sessions had not done the trick. This time, I would fly to Los Angeles to work on them at Raphael Saadiq's Blakeslee studio in North Hollywood. She would be in L.A. working on her supergroup's record at a nearby studio and would be able to drop by to oversee my progress. Any semblance of collaboration between us was over. She was in charge, and I was hers to manage and produce. Now that I was signed to her label, that seemed even more true.

We did photos for our album cover in that early stretch of the Los Angeles days. I had made our dresses for the shoot. They were part of the collection we'd (I'd) designed and built. They were similar shapes but had different details. They were both floor-length silk charmeuse dresses with empire waists and long sashes. Hers was lemon yellow, strapless, with tall hand-painted red tulips climbing up the skirt and a kelly green sash. Mine was a black halter top with white daisies growing up the skirt and a magenta sash. In the photos, we look like sisters. Her hair and makeup people made us look like her. I'm in there somewhere, but it's harder to detect. Some metaphors need not be made; they're literal, and there are pictures to prove it.

The first person who was hired to produce my vocals in Los Angeles was someone she had worked with on one of her solo albums. The guy showed up to the studio, told me how much he disliked her, and said he'd actually co-written one of her already-released songs but hadn't been given credit for it; he'd only been given credit for arranging the backing vocals. I only saw him that one time. To my knowledge, he left and did not return. So, there I was in Saadiq's studio, alone.

Again, the engineer I knew was hired. He came up from San Diego and he and I stayed at the same hotel during our time there. It was just the two of us in the studio again. She did come by every few days after her own daily session had wrapped. Her attention span wasn't what we hoped for given the amount of work we were doing every day, but it was a better system than waiting for her feedback from England while we sat around.

There were other things about the record that needed work in my opinion. The bass tracks had all been done with an acoustic bass in England. On fully produced, full band tracks, it sounded thin and weird; there was no sustain. Also, some of the guitar work needed help. Saadiq's studio was beautiful, but he wasn't around, and we'd been told that we weren't allowed to use the instruments that were there. I hadn't brought any of my guitars with me to Los Angeles because I thought I'd be solely focusing on vocals. I had a friend in Los Angeles who had a bunch of gear. He was the lead guitarist for Nine Inch Nails. They were in rehearsals for an upcoming tour in a studio not far from us. He was willing to lend me whatever I needed.

The engineer and I went over to where NIN were rehearsing, said hello to my friend, and were taken to his arsenal of instruments that were there at his disposal. An assistant helped us go through and find an electric bass and a couple of guitars to borrow for the week. We finally had a few tools with which to make this monster of a record sound a little more glued together.

Even then, it was interesting to me that I was being singled out as the only contributor whose parts needed work. That simply wasn't true. Everyone's parts were a little slanted, uneven, and disjointed, including hers. The England sessions had been a mess. But the narrative had already been set in motion by the loudest among us, and so it was. As we replaced the guitar and bass parts, she didn't even notice.

The engineer and I kept working. We were committed to making it work, to wrapping it up. I wrote the final song for our record during those sessions, a quiet song called "Any Color That You Want." Joss liked it. The engineer recorded a demo version of me playing and singing it while we were there, a placeholder for whatever she would end up doing with it. It was the sixteenth song.

I sang with all that I had that week. I had everything to prove—to her, to the engineer who had long been a harsh critic of my singing, and to myself. I did do my actual best, something I have not always been able to report. But I was starting to peel away from the project, and I could feel it. I was losing interest. The bar kept moving, and I knew that sometimes you just don't make it. It's not about you; it's about the abusive person waving the bar around.

After a week, we wrapped what we could, said our goodbyes and all went home.

There is one photo of me from the Los Angeles sessions. I'm in the tracking room sitting on a tall chair, holding a black acoustic guitar in front of a mic. I'm wearing pink jeans, red open-toed platform shoes, and a torn-up Siouxsie and the Banshees t-shirt held together by safety pins. My hair is up and I'm smiling at the camera. Pretty woman, pretty picture.

Hard time.

* * *

By the time she was telling me that my vocals still weren't good enough, I was in another space. I was in resistance. This time, she wanted me to work with a ridiculous guy I had met more than a year before, in Nashville. He was her friend and occasional collaborator. The year before, he had hit on me and later sent me a mix CD that included several overly emotional songs, only one of which I liked ("Anyday" by Any DiFranco). He was a typical white guy who thought very highly of himself, the type who rattles off their accomplishments and credits in the first thirty minutes you're around them. The kind that feels entitled to making out with you. The kind that thinks they know best how your songs and vocals should go.

Pass.

It was one thing to re-approach the vocals in the interest of making the best record we could. It was quite another to assume that the way to do that was to hire literally any man (and this guy truly was any and every man) and make him the leader. I had just enough self-respect to see it for what it was.

I said no. And she raged.

I had never said exactly no to her before. I had made requests and asked questions. I had shut down and gotten small. I had been quiet. But I hadn't said no. I got to see what happened when you said no to someone who was used to hearing yes. Linda Blair from *The Exorcist* comes to mind. There were emails, threats, insults, conference calls with both lawyers on the line, and finally:

"You're just not good enough to sing your own songs."

And there it was. The insult to end all insults, to raze all structures, to sever all ties. I would not get small. I would not circle back and pretend. I would quietly whisper "*fuck off*" in my own home, inaudible to anyone else. And I would leave the relationship.

I asked to be released from my deal with her. It took another several months, but eventually, I was free. She ended up making it sound as though parting ways had been her idea, ever the egoist. But it hadn't been. I asked. There's a paper trail.

* * *

That same season, I got a call from the Recording Academy. There had been a mistake, they said. I was more than willing to believe that the Grammy had been an error. But it was something else. A minor oversight had been made. Because I was co-producer of "This Little Light of Mine," I was being given a second Grammy. As a producer. That 7 AM tracking experience—that one-mic recording—had made me a Grammy winner. Twice.

The award certificates came in the mail later in the year. They're in an envelope somewhere in my office. I have never looked at them again. It's not because I'm not proud of being a Grammy winner. I am. But that experience was damaging. If I scrape my memories for the whole story, I do fondly remember writing with her, laughing, taking the day off and going into town to get our nails painted. I remember the hope, the thrill of singing together, and of not being able to tell which voice was mine. I remember waking her up to say goodbye when one of my flights back to Nashville was early in the morning; I remember hugging her in her bed, half asleep. I had loved her a little in the beginning. I had loved the opportunity to make something new. I had loved the idea of working with a woman.

But nothing will ever cloud the memory of that one sentence. Sometimes it has to get that bad to be able to see a thing for what it is, and then you can't unsee it. You shouldn't.

* * *

Our album was never released. Most of the time, I'm glad about it, though it remains the only record I've ever made that's been shelved. All that time and nothing to show for it. Most people in my life don't know that it even happened. I couldn't find the words for a long time. My lawyer was one of the only people who knew the whole story, and years later, he introduced me to someone at a party and said, "This is Buick Audra; she and I survived something together."

She kept the clothing line as well as the master sessions for the record. I kept my one dress with the daisies. I also have most of the music files; they're on a hard drive in a folder called WHO CARES. I didn't even want her name on anything in the end. But I've never been able to bring myself to delete the sessions. I'm in there, too, whatever else may be true. For as much as I've hated parts of myself in my lifetime, I've been hesitant to delete them altogether. I believe in the evidence of existence.

A few years ago, someone at a Nashville publishing company asked for some examples of my songwriting, both as a solo writer and in collaboration with other people. I decided to include two of the songs from that record, though they had never been properly mixed, and I hadn't heard them in years. I booted up the hard drive and set about mixing them myself. I could finally mute the goddamned rainstick. I picked two of the least offensive tracks from the collection, two that had actually been borne of our collaboration, not just our clashing wills and styles, and I listened.

I was surprised to hear what was there. The songs were lovely. We sounded lovely. *I* sounded lovely. It hadn't been about my vocals after all. It had been about power. It made me sad, but it also gave me peace. It had just been human bullshit all along, nothing more.

In a dark way, it reminded me of a scene from a horror film. In Karyn Kusama's *The Invitation*, a dinner party goes terribly wrong, and by the end of the evening, people are fighting for their own lives. There are no monsters or undead beings, only other party attendees and some truly bad ideas. In one scene, a man and woman are weighing their chance of survival if they dare to make a run for it. Some of their enemies are still alive and might be waiting in any number of places to slice them to ribbons. The man looks at the woman and says, "They are just people."

Just people.

Indeed.

Definition of *voice*

noun

3

an instrument or medium of expression

Five

Our apartment only has windows at one end. The front of the building is where all the light gets in. In the summer months, the leaves of a proud tree fill the view. In winter, on very clear days, you can see all the way across the water to the Statue of Liberty. That was a selling point when they rented it to us. I would have taken it without that, though. The apartment's primary appeal for me was that it wasn't in Boston.

Two days after we moved in here, he left on tour. He was gone the rest of the summer and most of the fall. I essentially moved to Brooklyn on my own, which I had been ready to do earlier in the year. I had said to him, "I'm moving to New York," and he had coyly asked, "Can I come?" It wasn't a given that he would come. We had spent so much time apart in the months and years leading up to my decision to move, all I knew was that I was going.

Boston had become like clothes that were two sizes too small: uncomfortable and uncompromising. It was time.

I unpacked this place and set it up alone. If he had preferences about what went where, it was beside the point. He wasn't here. We could figure that out later. I had to find a job and make new friends.

Friends. What a concept.

Our apartment is in the South end of Park Slope, on 18th Street between 5th and 6th Avenues. The huge building at the bottom of our street is a live/workspace for artists; the neighborhood is filled with families and people of all stripes, and there's a coffee shop a half block away called Has Beans. I love it. You can be brand new in a new place. No one knows your ex-best friend Jodi led a social destruction campaign against you, no one's concerned about the state of your marriage, and nobody cares about your old band's sad limp to the finish line. Newness is a gift. It paints over the grief. For a while, anyway.

We were new once.

I wrote a song last night. It might be the best song I've written to date. I wrote about how we met, how I felt when we got married, and how I feel now. I feel unsure.

I have been married for five years today, and I'm alone. The song gave way to arguing, which gave way to distance, and now he's chosen to spend the day in the city, recording. I'm left to my own choices again. About today, about tomorrow, about all of it.

It's September. The leaves of the tree in our front window are still plentiful but they're starting to change. If I peer between them, I can see Lady Liberty today.

She never wavers, but the visibility sure does.

* * *

When I was a non-smoking twenty-three-year-old, I worked at a hundred-something-year-old tobacco shop in Harvard Square, in Cambridge, MA. The shop was right across from Harvard Yard and attracted all kinds of human beings, from visiting celebrities to professors, to unhoused local folks. I was still in college because I didn't start school until I was twenty. Everyone else who worked there was in their twenties, too, with the exception of the owner. I have never known Paul's age and likely never will. He was maybe in his forties then, but if he was, it looked different on him. Paul had a personal rigidity that beckoned an earlier era. He was like someone out of the 1940s in his starched suiting and hard-heeled dress shoes. But the rest of us? Motley.

One of the women I worked with had a boyfriend who was in a band. I was in a band myself, so I wasn't impressed by that sort of qualifier, but she was. On a very cold day in January, I was at the counter with a pair of hot pink sparkly leggings tied around my neck in lieu of a scarf; my brother had borrowed my actual scarf to impress a woman that day. Two guys walked in to say hello to my co-worker; they were members of her boyfriend's band. I knew one of them. He and I chatted while the other one smiled at me from across the counter. We met, they left, and life went on.

I later learned that the smiling one said to the other, as they walked out:

"I'm going to marry her."

There was something familiar about him, an energy, a style. Our love was fast and shiny. We did everything too quickly and we did it in high gloss. Before him, I had spent more than a year dating someone who was prone to meanness and jealousy, who made dramatic visual art about me and hung it in local venues for our entire scene to behold. This guy was nothing of the sort. He was happy, excited, and he lit up around me. His friends remarked that they'd never seen him act that way around a woman. I took it all in as positive omens, as definitions of love. I was ready for whatever adventure certainly awaited us.

By May, we were living together. I was thrown into a fully formed scene of people who looked like they worked very hard at being cool. Most of them wore vintage denim and had impeccable mod haircuts. Some of them even had Vespas. I was not part of that scene or any other retro movement. I listened to Mariah Carey and Soundgarden and had hair like Barbie—on purpose. But because I was with him, they accepted me into the fold, though I would remain an outlier in more ways than one.

That time in our lives is chronicled in Polaroids and photo booth strips. We never took a bad picture together. We went dancing several nights a week, laughed, listened to music, and we did it all out loud. The memories exist like a cross-processed indie film you've only seen once but sort of remember the gist of. I was the leading woman who had come from abuse and dysfunction, but who now had a high ponytail and a resilient attitude. People love when women use the word *resilient*; it means we don't have to talk about it.

When he proposed after a year, I accepted. When it was time to plan a wedding, I threw my whole self into it. I was good at all of that: creating things, planning, being the boss, and making everything look fantastic from the outside. I was like a one-woman PR firm for my own life.

In the beginning, we both mattered. We both played music, we both had friends and other communities around us, and we both came from something. He came from a family that was Polish on one side and Irish on the other—Catholic all around. Almost all of his relatives lived in Massachusetts, and most of them lived quite close together. I came from three parents, one of whom had stopped calling when I was fifteen. My family was Catholic on one side, too, but I wasn't. I was the child of the lapsed Catholic in the family and the agnostic former stepfather figure. My people lived all over hell's half acre and were rarely in the same room together—if ever. I branded it as Bohemian.

I knew how to act. I knew how to make myself shiny despite my lifelong markings. After all, I'd been living in camouflage all along. There was an internal, unspoken contract with myself that seeming fine was equal to being fine, and I could make that happen.

* * *

He was in a band. The band was five white guys. They had a catchy name and a lot of curb appeal. He wrote the majority of the songs with one other guy, who happened to be the one I already knew. I liked being with another songwriter. It's a shared dialect within the broader language of music. There's something about the ability to produce music that previously only existed in your mind that is akin to sorcery.

I was in a band, too. My band was three people total, and clearly, we were not all men. The other two members of my band were guys, though. We were a post-punk, driving, weirdo rock band that wrote angular songs and played in town a lot. I was the primary songwriter, as well as the guitarist and vocalist. Head sorcerer.

His band was a punk band. They had a sort of "Rah-Rah" anthemic thing going on that borrowed heavily from the Ramones, but also Stiff Little Fingers and a few other man bands. In their world, it was almost as though women had never made music. Maybe they didn't even exist. No, wait, they existed to be on album covers and in videos, but outside of that: it was Manville.

As such, our projects did not coexist within the same scene. Boston had a whole punk scene dedicated to bands like his, and my band existed among the other weirdo groups of less-defined genres—and of varied genders. My scene had women.

At the time of our meeting, his band was being signed to a prominent indie label. They were being signed off of a demo. The first month that we knew each other, they recorded their debut LP for the label.

It was an exciting time for them. It was all very intense and forever-feeling. And just as swiftly as he entered my life, he left it. Getting signed and releasing the album took him away on tour for several months of that first year. I thought it was great. I have never been one to think folks have to be together all the time. I was happy about his sudden success and momentum with his art.

What I didn't anticipate was how used to being on my own I would become. We were apart for easily six months of every year—more as time went on. He was gone until two days before our wedding, to which he had invited ninety of his own family members. That math is intense, even now. Built into that math was an expectation that I would handle it. Not for us, but for him. And I did.

Eventually, there was a major label deal. His band had been on a farewell tour when a bidding war broke out among a few majors, and so they stayed together. The band getting signed to a major upped the ante quite a bit. It would become the only thing in his life, and it was fairly central to mine, too. I was expected to be a Band Wife, a plus-one to his existence.

All along, I was playing my own music. I was making records, collaborating with people, and doing my thing. But it became quite secondary, and not just by him. What I have learned out here, is that being a woman standing near or next to literally any man— could be anyone at all—immediately makes her smaller. I walked right into that quicksand. Everyone launched into that behavior with me. What was *he* doing? Where was *he* touring? When was *his* record coming out? In the beginning, I answered them, but later I got very used to saying, "I don't know; ask him."

Women do not exist to report on the men they know. Write it down.

It's amazing how much space someone can take up, even when they're absent. My entire identity morphed into being his partner. His family had expectations of me, my family had expectations of me, and our friends had expectations of me. I wish I could tell you that I told them all to fuck off, but instead, I told myself to fuck off. I ran around doing everything for everyone. I became unwell and un-me.

Four years in, I decided I was moving to New York. Boston no longer felt like it held anything for me, and I was essentially living alone. He was now gone for something like nine months per year. If I was going to live alone, I wanted to live somewhere else, somewhere better. Brooklyn was better. It was at least a second chance. The possibility of starting over with people who might not see me as less than half of a whole was greatly appealing. And for him, it was just another place to leave his stuff. Eventually, some of his band members followed us, and before long, he had replicated his entire scene around us again.

Brooklyn marked the end of my time in 33 Slade. After eight years, my brother dove headlong into a lifestyle that would later catch up with him, our bassist moved to Seattle, and I was just . . .

On my own. Right.

I did what women who find themselves alone have been doing since the dawn of time: I made a solo record.

Two weeks after moving into our third-floor apartment in South Park Slope, I drove to Maryland to record an eight-song EP with Matt Squire, the engineer who had recorded the second album by my now defunct band. He had moved away from Boston, too, back to his home state. I made *Rose Ink* over the course of two days. The entire record is me playing my 1960 Fender Duo-Sonic and singing. That's it. Matt messed around on the computer while I belted out my saddest, solo-est truths for all the mics to hear.

Rose Ink was created without any outside input, which was a relief at the time. I didn't have anyone in my ear telling me about my pitch or my guitar playing. For that reason, my performances live in this wildly un-self-conscious space. I don't believe that we make art for only ourselves, but *Rose Ink* is as close to an audible journal entry as I've ever made. My vocals are virtually untouched on the record; they sound exactly as my voice does when I sing by myself.

I didn't put the record out for two years. I had recorded it to hear what I sounded like at that moment, at that juncture. A musical snapshot. But I hated it at the time. Oddly, my husband loved it. He got a tattoo of the cover (granted, Scott Campbell had hand-drawn the art). My husband had once told me that 33 Slade just wasn't his thing, a casually cruel statement that gutted me at the time. It was interesting that he claimed to love my music without the power of the band, without the confidence of my other writing. *Interesting* might not be the word.

When I started making *Singer*, everything shifted. It was the first time in our entire relationship that my music had caused prolonged travel. It was also the first time I'd bet on myself as an actual artist, separate from being in a band or other collaborative efforts. And I didn't care what anyone thought about it. I had been working for two years straight and paying the majority of our bills doing work I had never intended to do. I was ready to invest in my own art again. I couldn't afford to record the way his project did; I didn't have a big budget provided by a label. I had a somewhat surprising career as a designer for people of some notoriety. I was making more than I ever had, but I was also paying for more.

Singer was a mixture of truths and wishes. I was telling pretty stories about things that begged a closer look, but at least that was only part of the project's narrative. In many ways, the album serves as a fairly accurate document of the marriage itself. On the first track, a song called "The Intangible," I'm claiming a forever love, one that I would never leave. And by the last track, "One Good Year," I'm admitting that things aren't so solid and that it's likely time for me to carve out a road of my own. Did he hear it? Did I? Hard to say. But I hear it now.

We tried. He tried, I tried, and we tried. Whatever strange assortment of tools we each possessed didn't add up to a working set. Resentment and loneliness grew, and I started to have questions; not just about him, either. About me, too. I was easily emotionally distracted. Anyone who paid my music the slightest bit of attention was like a dream to me. It was easy to wonder what it might be like to also matter, to be heard. As far as the questions I had about him, I wrote them down one night.

Baby, how about you?
Do the miles of road ever get old?
And are you ever blue?
'Cuz honey, to tell you the truth
I've been feeling kind of borrowed
Almost never new
But baby, how about you?

* * *

I spent the summer after finishing *Singer* in Nashville, renting a room from a woman who was like something out of a documentary about the aftermath of extreme religions. She talked about having spoken in tongues at her church. I stayed in my room when she and I were both at home. I was uninterested in knowing more about that.

I'd initially gone to Tennessee on the recommendation of Doug Sax earlier in the season. I booked a one-way flight, rented a car, and went to see what he was talking about. Nashville was a bit of a mythological place to me, a collection of addresses for recording studios and home to a couple of people I knew from my work in fashion. Doug had put in a call to an engineer who made high-profile bluegrass records and also worked for a label. He wanted us to meet. We met the second day I was in town. I met other people, too, in random, serendipitous ways. It felt like the yellow brick road was unfolding before me.

My husband was going to be gone for much of the summer, his band was doing another farewell tour; they had finally decided to hang it up. In an uncharacteristic move on my part, I offered to come out for some of the West Coast dates (I did not believe in touring with a partner; it seemed like the stuff of groupies), but he waved me off. He said he thought it would be best if I didn't come. I went to Nashville instead. Besides, I had just wrapped my album with a song about finding a road of my own. Maybe this was it.

The summer was wild and full. I met dozens and dozens of people, all musicians, save for my perhaps fundamentalist roommate and one hair stylist who went to every single show on the East side of town. It was intoxicating and encouraging. No one knew my old life. Again, I was new. A chance at being seen, at being heard. Plus, I was playing and writing all the time. Finally.

I left at the end of August. I drove straight to Philadelphia where my partner was playing the second-to-last of his band's shows. Half of the band was originally from Philly, so it was a hometown show for them. The next night would be at the Knitting Factory in New York. The last show. It was a huge deal for him; I wouldn't have missed it.

There's a photo of us from the Philly show that paints such a vibrant story. The band is playing a song that my husband wrote, and which I arranged and sang backing vocals for on the album. I'm standing on stage at a mic wearing short black shorts and an oversized pink t-shirt with his band's logo emblazoned across the front. He's playing guitar and beaming at me, and I'm singing with my whole body, one hand to my ear. It's a dazzling image. We were good for that.

But things were off. Secrets and chatter swirled around the room. People I knew were crying, couples were fighting, and I was out of the loop. No one wanted to know how my summer in Nashville had been. There, in that world, I was a wife again. On duty. But I had questions. Lots of questions. I smiled through it—I played my part—but I asked later.

Sometimes when you ask, you find out. You might not find out right away, but eventually, the truth pokes through and floods the room with light.

And you will leave the Statue of Liberty where you found her. You will wonder why you never went to visit her. You lived there for four whole years, and you never once went to see her *or* the Empire State

Building. And by the way, had you noticed the changing of the seasons in real time, or had it occurred all around you while you scurried in and out of subway stations, keeping your little life scotch-taped together? Too late. You can come back and do those things like the tourist you'll someday be, and you'll never come back to this street.

It will remain a memory and a Polaroid, ever fading.

Deadbolt

He's sitting across from me, smiling. He approves of everything I'm saying—everyone does. I'm doing it again. I'm making a bad story good; making it all okay for the audience, even an audience of one. I'm aware that I'm doing it, but it's hard to stop doing something that other people like. It becomes a way of life after a while.

He's in town with his wife and two small children; they've come to see the rising spectacle that is Nashville these days. They're staying at a hotel downtown. He and I are at Crema, at a table in the back by the bathrooms. There was only so much ground to cover in our own lives. Now we're in the Catching-Up-About-My-Ex portion of the hang, and I'm playing my well-worn part. After all, he is an old friend of my ex's; that's how he and I know each other in the first place. I'm telling stories about what good friends my former spouse and I

have become in the years since I left, talking about how I'm still in contact with all of my former in-laws. And it's all true.

He approves.

* * *

I didn't tell many people why I left. My parents and brother knew, as did maybe four of my closest friends. Right before I moved away, I called one of his sisters and told her, so someone on the other side would know. I loved his sisters. I loved his whole family. But I was leaving. It felt as though the reason didn't even belong to me. His story wasn't mine to tell.

It's tricky to tell one half of a story. It's like showing someone one half of a painting and assuming it's enough for the viewer. But it was what I did.

I never thought I'd leave that marriage. I would never have made the shell pink silk dupioni wedding gown, all the bridesmaids' dresses, his vest, and all the groomsmen's vests if I thought I might. It would have been easier to open a clothing boutique instead. I was in it—as much as I knew how to be, which turned out to be not very much. I didn't have a lot of experience with marriage. None of my parents had ever been married to each other and I was the first of my friends to get hitched. It was a wild guess wrapped in hope, protected by youth for as long as that lasted. One day, it fell spectacularly apart.

To be fair, I didn't exactly decide to leave. One day I was in the relationship, I came into some information, and the next thing I knew, I was leaving. It wasn't anger or punishment. It was worse. It was the realization that I'd never known him at all, and that he hadn't known me. There was no discussion to be had, there were merely things to sort out and keys to be turned in. It was like a sidewalk ending and falling to another life. Over.

You know you're really leaving when you're looking at houses alone in another state, a thousand miles away. I was going.

* * *

Two months earlier, we had spent New Year's Eve in Philadelphia. His new band was based out of Philly, and they were playing a local NYE show. The wife of the band's lead singer was standing next to me for most of the set. In those circles, it was assumed that the women would all know each other, simply because we were women. But this woman was an office manager with a teenager at home. I was a musician and artist myself. We had nothing in common other than these two men who happened to be collaborators and who shared a first name. Still, I was toeing the line in a marriage that observed such rules.

She kept pointing to my husband and saying, "Look at him! Isn't he *soooooo* cute?"

I didn't get it. Why was this woman campaigning for me to think my own husband was cute? Because I wasn't a gushing fangirl? I'd seen him play on stage hundreds of times by then. I thought he was great. I had shown that over the years we had spent together, but it didn't seem to be enough for her that night.

After I left the marriage, I began to understand that those people had known a different person than I had. He had shown them someone else. Or maybe he'd shown *me* someone else. Either way, a duality had transpired. A story had been told in one direction or another.

It turned out that I had been living with missing information all along. There had been signs. There was the time he called from tour to tell me he wasn't coming home the next day after all, that the band was jumping on another tour instead, and that he had just found out about it. There was the time he came home from tour with none of his belongings. Like, nothing. Not his guitar, not our camera, not his clothing; nothing. Stories were told and lies were spun. I found his existence bizarre and questionable, but I wasn't the kind of partner who investigated their spouse. His whole identity was wrapped up in these behaviors.

Everyone else loved his "flaky" ways. But everyone else wasn't married to him. I was.

* * *

We stayed friends for years. I liked him much more once we weren't married to each other, once I had no needs. There's something about the removal of expectation that allows for a different observation and appreciation. I found him funny and kind, both qualities that had been obscured by my own confusion and disappointment when we were together. I was in Nashville, and he was still in Brooklyn. We even played some shows together when I was on tour alone. We went back to his hometown together once or twice and showed up at some family events as friends. It was The Great Success that had risen from the ashes. Everyone thought so. Almost everyone.

When my band Friendship Commanders was asked to open for one of his band's reunion shows in New York City, we happily accepted. We were still fairly new, grateful for the opportunity of potential exposure to a much larger audience. He and I had been on good terms for a long time by then; it seemed fine. It wasn't until I walked backstage before the show and saw someone from his old scene that I understood how off I was. It was pure ice. It was incredulous and it was pure ice. The kind of energy that says, *I can't believe you've actually shown up to this.*

I realized in that moment that *I* hadn't told anyone why I had left, *but neither had he.* And so, in the absence of a reason, and in the absence of me, a story had been formed. I was the wayward woman who'd run off to . . . what? Do what they had been doing all along? Make records and play shows and do whatever the hell I wanted?

Yes. But it looks different on a woman.

I got that response several times throughout that night, from all kinds of people. In hindsight, I can't believe I wasn't prepared for it. I had gone such a wildly different way when we split, I truly believed he had done the same. I wouldn't allow anyone to speak ill of him in my presence. I was carrying around a story of total mutual respect following the split. I really could have been a PR person. I've spun a lot of things in my time.

After that night, our friendship remained intact, but I was aware that things were different. The following year, our friendship finally ended because of a very simple boundary I set around a collaboration he asked me to do with him while I was on tour. He kept moving the location and when I wouldn't accommodate the change of venue (the difference being Western Massachusetts and Asbury Park, New Jersey), he had a bad reaction. It's amazing what finally sinks a ship. Sometimes they manage to float after collision with a glacier, and other times a small leak sends the whole enterprise overboard.

It was as surprising as it was okay. We'd given it enough shots. Sometimes endings are just endings; they don't need more definition than that. And maybe I didn't need to keep everything afloat forever. I had a long history of trying to make things work past their expiration date, believing on a cellular level that if I couldn't, I was the problem. It was time to let that go.

* * *

The next year, an old Boston friend came to Nashville on tour, and I took him out to dinner before his show. We were catching up about all the folks we had in common when he said something that turned my head ever so slightly. He didn't see it; he was looking down at his food, still talking. He was talking about my ex. He was saying something about another behavior that had occurred during my marriage. Something he thought I knew. I didn't.

I didn't say anything.

But it turned out that I had truly never known the man I had once called my husband. And what's more, all of those people who were always around my husband, in his band, in his other communities—they all knew. They knew and they let me make the banana bread for the tours, they let me take care of everything, and they treated me like I was some unwitting war bride who didn't need to know the truth about the gritty front line. They stopped just short of patting me on the head.

If misogyny were an Olympic sport, these people would be on the team representing the United States of America, proudly. And they would win.

* * *

I don't tend to watch awards shows. Once you've seen how the sausage gets made, the sausage show holds decidedly less appeal. But I made myself watch the clip. I had to, just once. I had to see it with my own eyeballs.

He wore a tux. He got dressed in a tuxedo and still managed to look damp. She looked like royalty, of course. Nothing about that was surprising. But there *he* was, his heavy-lidded eyes drooping as he stood slightly behind her. The Feminist and the Fraud, on stage at the Oscars. Unbelievable.

My social media has been abuzz with excitement and congratulatory posts from all kinds of people I used to know, praising his success while scrambling to align themselves with it. A few of them know what he did to me, too. And yet, there they are, acting like he's a global ambassador of goodwill.

It's a good day to let people go.

* * *

Before we got married, we went to another wedding, in May of that same year. Two friends of ours got hitched, a pair of photographers. Everyone we knew from my partner's world was there. It was a de facto Scene Wedding. I was never a proper member of said Scene, even when I was in good standing due to proximity to one of its members. Still, I was invited, and we went.

There's a photo of me from that day. The bride took it. It's a portrait from when we first arrived, of just my head and shoulders. I'm cheated to the side but I'm looking right at the camera, smiling a wide, true smile. I liked the bride. She was cool and she took excellent photos. I was happy to be there. My then-finance is behind me in the image, ghosty and out of focus. It hadn't happened yet.

The ceremony was in a family member's back yard, but we went to an event hall for the reception, a 1970s building that looked like it might have once been a library. It had an upper level for tables and dancing, and then a basement level where the bathrooms and water fountains were located.

Among the many guests in attendance was a guy I'd known for about as long as I'd known my partner. They belonged to the same social group. He was another man in a band that we were all supposed to care about; I didn't think they were any good, but nobody ever asked me what I thought. He and I had been friendly when we first met, but there had been an air of flirtatiousness that wasn't right for me at the time. I chose my fiancé. After that, the guy and I merely co-existed.

I made several trips to the bathroom on the day of that wedding, and one time, this guy also happened to be downstairs. He backed me up against a wall and leaned into me, his face so close to mine that his spit hit my skin as he spoke. He was sweaty, angry looking, and pinning my arms to my sides.

He said, "You know what you are? You're a super person, and I would never fuck a super person. Who wants to fuck a super person?" He was glaring at me, but his mouth was smiling. I could feel my heartbeat in my eyeballs. It was as though he was picking up a conversation that had begun at an earlier time, except, that conversation had never happened between us. He repeated versions of those lines a few times like he was trying to get them just right.

Meanwhile, people were going up and down the stairs. I saw a woman I knew named Joanna. She looked right at us and proceeded to walk up the stairs.

Was this the way other people behaved at weddings? Did this seem normal to her or anyone else?

He slowly moved off of me and wandered away. I made my way back upstairs to the party. I found my partner and tried to describe what had just transpired. The look on his face was not one of reaction or anger, but instead, it was one of, *please be quiet, we're in public*. I was aware that we were in public; that was part of what had made the whole encounter so appalling. My partner didn't want to talk about it, then or later.

I told the married couple, too, months after the fact. After all, wouldn't reasonable people want to know that such a thing had happened at their otherwise joyous event? I thought so, but no. He was part of their inner circle, a close friend. It was chalked up to too much alcohol, to circumstance. He was a good guy, they said, it was just a bad moment.

Was this what life was? Excusing incredible behavior under the banner of Bad Moments? I'd been down this road before, the road of being the only one saying *this is immensely fucked up.* It seemed to always come down to me having to get over a thing. And here I was, being asked to do it again.

I never got over it, but I did put it away. Once we all scattered from Boston, that became easier to do. Unbelievably, I ran into him at another wedding three years later, this time in Philadelphia. I arrived late because I was coming from a television taping in Manhattan, so I snuck into the ceremony and sat where I could find an open seat. He was seated directly behind me. I felt my whole body react when I saw him. I had forgotten for a while, but my body had not. When our eyes met, I said, "Don't come anywhere near me. Don't even look at me." The people around us heard it.

Good, I thought. *Let people hear a woman speak for herself. Let people have a reason to take note that something is not right, for once.*

He moved to England and became something of a name after that. Who cares. I never did. It wasn't until he co-wrote the song for that movie that I paid attention. When I saw them all praise and congratulate him, I paid attention for the first time in years. Mostly, I was watching them, the same group who had so easily blamed me for the end of my marriage but had been able to excuse all questionable behavior by the dudes with no problem at all.

The men and their music, the center of their universe. It had always been their religion; why did I ever expect it to be otherwise? Why had I ever bothered with any of them in the first place? And why was I surprised to still not matter at all?

After the Oscars, I let the whole group of them go. Sometimes it's okay to be the outsider. Sometimes exclusion is a compliment.

* * *

I carried guilt for a long time after I left my marriage. I felt like I had failed; failed him, myself, our families, everyone. But the truth is that I was failing myself when I was there. I was also failing myself when I told the good story, the one everyone liked. Who did it ever help? It never helped me.

Sometimes I'll mention that I'm divorced, and the other person will look at me like they're sorry to hear it. I like to clear that up when I can. Now, whenever I get the opportunity, I tell the truth right out loud. And the honest truth is:

I'm so glad I left.

Definition of *voice*

noun

4

a

wish, choice, or opinion openly or formally expressed

b

right of expression

also : influential power

The Tendencies

Today would have been my grandmother's birthday. There's a picture of her with me as a baby next to where I'm sitting in my office at home. She was already legally blind then, but she made things with her hands right to the end of her life. She was a knitter who made each of us four cousins a twin-sized blanket when we were born and kept us in hand-knit cuddle-mocs that she called "bunnies" as we grew into adults. But, in her younger years, long before any of us existed, she studied voice in college, a noteworthy detail in the life of a woman from her generation.

I inherited the music and the desire to work with my hands. I inherited other things, too.

* * *

I once released an album that took three years, more money than was available, and a pound of flesh to make. As a gift to myself, I released it the day before my birthday. It was my second attempt to do such a thing, and my second album as a solo artist. A swing and a miss both times. It was called *Family Album*. My idea was to include as many members of my families of origin and choice as I could. I extended an offer to my immediate loved ones to contribute songs if they felt so moved. I wanted to record the whole thing in homes, no studios. It was a big old dream that I took seriously for a long old time. It's a good album. It also didn't need to be as difficult as it was.

Toward the end of working on my first solo album, *Singer*, my brother was arrested in Massachusetts. I started working on *Family Album* later that year so that I could include him before he served his prison sentence. I even had a filmmaker friend document the process. The pending incarceration infused the sessions with urgency, immediacy, and grief and I have it recorded on both audio and visual mediums. The first sessions were at his then-home in Somerville,

Massachusetts. The people included were my brother Boey, our mother, Nate Edgar (bassist and friend), my then-husband, and my co-producer at the time. The sessions took place over three days of back-to-back blizzards.

The second sessions were done in my home in Nashville, fifteen months after those three days in Somerville. The people included were all non-relatives, all family of choice. It was lighter, easier, and decidedly less intense.

The third and final sessions were at the home of my brother's father, in Miami, Florida. The house was one that my brother and I had partially grown up in together. It was also where I'd lived for two and a half years of my adolescence when my mother moved me out of her home in Boston. Much time had passed since then and I wanted to extend the project to that branch of the family. The offer was accepted, and I arranged for my co-producer to fly from San Diego to our former hometown. I would drive down from Nashville with all of the gear. The goal was to record as many members of that family as we could, in addition to my mom's sister and a few other longtime family friends.

Life had other things in store.

* * *

When I was a kid, we spent the summers in the North woods of Wisconsin. My mom's family has had a place there for over a hundred years on a small body of water called Pelican Lake. My grandparents were there in the summers, as were my mom's three siblings and their kids. Most of my memories of those times are positive.

But I was often in trouble during those summers. My mother, the only single parent of the lot, often pinned her frustrations on me and I was regularly sent to the room I shared with my brother as a punishment. I spent entire days alone with no television or other distractions. I taught myself to sew up there. I spent countless hours sewing by hand, often making small, embroidered pillows for

my extended family members. I bet if you were to rummage around the dresser drawers of my now long-gone elders, you'd find at least one small pillow with a wobbly G stitched on one side. "G" for Granny and/or Grandpa. They were cute, but they were also the byproduct of punishment and isolation.

* * *

The Miami sessions were a baptism of fire. I didn't expect things to be easy; that wasn't the family's way. But I didn't expect the rage either.

There had been tension in the seasons before. My brother's arrest had thrown the family into the most honest versions of ourselves, as individuals and as a collective. Whatever we'd been before was stripped away and our true natures were exposed. As it turned out, our true natures weren't so compatible, even in the short term.

I had expressed grief and disappointment after the arrest. The family's lifestyle and choices had directly contributed to the situation. While I was aware that my brother was an autonomous person, we had been raised in unsafe environments with all kinds of criminal activity around us. I had verbalized my frustrations and since made amends, but right before the Miami sessions, I learned that the family wasn't satisfied. There had been emails and calls about how I owed additional apologies, and to whom. When I refused, I put myself in a space outside the family. That was made perfectly clear when I arrived.

I was expecting to stay at the house and record there for several days. My brother's father allowed it but informed me that no one from his branch of the family would be contributing to the project. There were four of them in total, but three of them were actually musicians. I was losing two good acoustic guitar players and a harpist. It appeared I'd driven a thousand miles for nothing. Nothing but a hostile recording environment and a new thing to live through. I couldn't afford to go anywhere else, so we proceeded.

My co-producer and I knew the house well. I had lived there when we were sweethearts as kids. We'd been back as adults a time or two, but the place was largely a set from the past that we, now adults, were performing in. The house was a rare two-story Craftsman-style structure set on several acres of mango and avocado groves. We'd been given permission to record in the upstairs back bedroom, which had been my brother's father's room when I lived there. He now spent the majority of his time at his partner's house in South Miami and slept downstairs in what used to be the den when he was at this house. This house was called the Brown House. Everyone who'd ever known my family called it that. We did, too.

The back upstairs room was isolated enough that we felt we could barricade ourselves in there and get the work done without having to be otherwise present or disruptive in the house. We ignored as many of the past and present ghosts as we could. We moved into hyper-productivity mode. We knew that mode. We'd already completed one of my albums by spending long days in the studio and ignoring reality. It was our shared way. In the absence of the family, we focused on building the remaining tracks ourselves and finishing the ones we'd built in the two previous sessions. Those sessions had rendered full band performances, and these would be guitar and vocal-focused. Fine.

My mother ended up being in town for the sessions, so we had her come by to sing. Her sister, my aunt Nancy, came by separately to contribute vocals as well. They'd already been estranged for years but are both terrific singers who sound remarkably alike.

* * *

There were reel-to-reel tapes in the living room at the Big House in Pelican Lake. We never got them out, but the adults would sometimes talk about how their grandfather Reese had recorded the girls singing "Mr. Sandman" by The Chordettes when they were children. My mother and her sister had learned the power of sister harmonies very

young. Their mother's tone was different from their clear, ice-water voices. Hers was lower, smokier. But all of them were born singers.

* * *

My mother's lifelong friend and collaborator Eddie Zyne came to the Brown House both to bring instruments we didn't have and to play percussion on a few tracks. Eddie had been a drummer for Hall & Oates in the 1970s, and he'd also been in bands with my mother and biological father before I was born. Eddie had been like an uncle to me for as long as I could remember. He played cajon on one track and sleigh bells on another, and also lent us his steel drum and baritone uke. My mother was happier when Eddie was around, younger seeming. Their friendship had endured quite a lot and they were still able to make each other laugh. It made me wonder if my co-producer and I could end up like that. Our relationship had started much younger, but we were still going all these years later. There was something about us that was different, though. We fell out for years at a time. My mom and

Eddie weren't like that. And it didn't seem like they had ever tried to change each other. We couldn't say the same.

We worked long days. My co-producer went back to his parents' house at night, and I stayed at the Brown House. We would occasionally encounter my brother's father and that went a number of different ways: rage, silence, sulking, and then finally, a visit. He came to the room once to see what kind of progress we were making. My co-producer took a couple of photos of us standing around playing guitars while listening to what we'd tracked, but he continued to sit out the project.

During those sessions, I sang the final lead vocals on all of the songs that were mine to sing. I'd become quite self-conscious about my pitch after making *Singer,* so I had taken to singing without headphones, to low monitor volume. Most of the vocals on *Family Album* are complete takes, unedited. I tracked one song written by my mother, one by my biological father, and one by Fred Neil, a person who had been like family during my childhood. My collaborator and I wrote the last song together, as we had done on the album before it. I wrote about being in that house and not feeling welcome. I wrote about how the grown man who had made the choice not to participate in the album would not be able to claim his absence as an exclusion. It had been his call. We are not victims of our own decisions.

We got through it. On the morning we left town, as we were leaving the driveway, I said, "I'm not coming back here." I was eating yogurt with a spoon from the house, something I'd accidentally taken without thinking. I still have the spoon, and I have never gone back.

* * *

I think I've made about fifteen baby quilts. Nieces, nephews, children of friends and co-workers, etc. The quilting started in my teens after I'd been sewing by hand for years. I got a machine when I was eighteen and my brother taught me how to use it. He had one, too, but he's never made anyone a blanket or a quilt. I'm not sure he's made

anyone anything. I liked sewing for a long time; I like it less now.

There's something about being expected to produce something that makes me not want to do it. There's also something about wasting time in this life. If you waste time, you don't have to try at what you're most afraid of doing. The thing that matters to you.

Did my grandmother love making those blankets, or did she feel obligated to make them? I should have asked her. I should have asked her about her music, too.

* * *

It took me two more years after the Miami sessions to finish and release *Family Album*. I signed my record deal with Joss while I was tracking it and she was technically entitled to the first refusal of its release—if I had told her about it, that is. I hadn't. She had that glimmer in her eye of delighting in taking away the thing you loved, so I kept it out of sight until I was released from my deal. My relationship with my longtime co-producer fell away, too, leaving the album as mine to finish alone, which I did. I had a few more people perform on it in Nashville, and then I did all of the editing myself. I mixed it with Eric McConnell over at his house/studio, and that was it.

It was momentous to finish it at all, never mind by myself. Somehow, I'd allowed a belief system to take root, one that told me I couldn't make things without someone else. It wasn't with me when I was younger; it had happened in my young adulthood and been reinforced along the way. Death of self-confidence by a thousand cuts. There were the mean-spirited comments from my mother; the lazy statements by other family members that credited everyone but me for my work; the dynamic with my first husband and the innate sexism built into that community; and my co-producer and his strange ideas about me. They had all happened. The worst betrayal, though, was my lack of faith in myself. I had just enough to keep myself going, to keep making the work, but too little to skip the partnerships, to skip the damage.

The other belief system that had to be examined and dismantled was the one that told me it was my job to create a better ending to any of the stories. That one had rooted itself much earlier—in fact, I don't remember a time without it. I had always felt like an extra piece, an inconvenience to the people in my life. My existence had been unplanned, my upbringing had been a burden, and I had been left by the people who were supposed to stick around—more than once. It's easy to see how I would have become a person who wanted to stick the landing, to get a winning score somewhere, somehow. And so, I made things, I gave things, and at my most extreme, I tried to bring everyone together for something I hoped would be beautiful.

Family Album is beautiful if you don't know much about it.

Some of the memories are lovely, too. Not the ones I expected. Oddly, it was the best collaborative experience I ever had with my co-producer. Right at the end, we got it together—on one level, at least. Even still, my guitar playing is conspicuously sparse on that album. That belief had wedged itself in there, too. Songs I had written entirely alone were played by my ex-husband or my co-producer. I'm in there, but much less than I should have been. I didn't allow him to beat me up with the vocals, but I did let the guitar get away from me. I regret it.

Some people think regret is toxic, a meaningless emotion we'd do well to avoid. I don't. I think regret is instructive. A warning that you crossed some threshold you ought not cross again, lest you find yourself on similar terrain once more. The things I did to myself around *Singer* and *Family Album*, I regret. Many parts of my life were beyond my control, but the things I had the power to do or not, I misjudged. I used to worry about the people I injured with my choices, but these days I think about how much I injured myself. Self-injury is the hardest to forgive, and the one we're least encouraged to heal from.

By the time *Family Album* came out, my mother had stopped speaking to me. In a moment of hopeful gratitude for being the only of my three parents to participate in the album, I dedicated the record to her. She ignored both its release and my birthday, which were on either side of a midnight. Worse than the dedication was my choice to include a photo of myself and my co-producer on the inside fold of the album, sitting back-to-back in the driveway of the Brown House. I have no excuse. Old habits die hard. *Be nice, be giving, and tell them a better story than it was.* Those tapes played loudly in my mind.

The very idea of not giving away what's mine is radical. Giving credit, giving dedication, and giving heart. Like stitches you labor over that no one ever looks at, but that they accept because they believe they deserve them. I want to feel like that. Like I am deserving. I'm fairly certain it's an inside job. Maybe it starts with giving less. If I kept it all, would I have more?

I'm willing to find out.

The Alcoholics Wish You Well

"They're not doing it to you, they're just doing it and you're in the way."

I'd love to believe it.

* * *

Sometimes it's a few months, sometimes it's years. When she stops speaking to me, I quietly prepare for it to be the last time, every time.

My mother didn't speak to me for three years when *Family Album* came out. In that window of time, I got remarried. Not in secret, nor in a hurry. No, I had a wedding with a lead-up and all of that. She held fast. I found out later that she called a friend of mine to make fun of me on my wedding day; tried to find some solidarity in poking fun at my decision to remarry. She did something like that the first time, too, and she was at that wedding.

The freeze started two months before *Family Album* was released. I decided to go back to Boston for Christmas. It was my brother's first holiday season since his release from prison and it seemed like I should be there. Plus, my partner still hadn't met Bo, even though we'd been dating for years and were by then engaged. Bo didn't want to meet anyone when he was still inside. Fair enough.

We got to Boston on Christmas Eve afternoon, a full day later than planned. My car had died for good on the drive up—at night, to boot. We lost a day of driving to getting it towed, renting a car, and transferring an unreasonable amount of stuff from one vehicle to the other.

When we got to town, we went straight to the bakery where my brother worked. He and my partner briefly met, and plans were discussed. We would be staying with him and his partner; but did they have food

142

for all of us? What could we contribute? My brother reported that he had made four apple pies and that they also had Brussels sprouts. He said they'd been eating a lot of Brussels sprouts.

I could feel it in my body. Every old, familiar feeling, back in full force—shame, chief among them. We had driven for days and would be fed Brussels sprouts. This man who wanted to marry me would finally know I was from the circus, and it would be announced by the lone presence of Brussels sprouts on a Christmas table.

I had chosen not to spend major holidays with either of my parents while my brother was in prison, so this was the first family holiday I'd attended in three years. I had forgotten all of this. I had forgotten that I had often done the work at the holidays. I had been the cook and host. I'd been the Good Girl.

We had about an hour left until stores would close for the holiday. We would have to rush in and out to get any kind of meal provisions together. We drove to a nearby Whole Foods. I called my mother, briefly forgetting that I wasn't from one of those families where you can lovingly complain about one family member to another in good fun. I told her my brother planned to serve Brussels sprouts and apple pies for Christmas, so we were out getting the rest. What did she want us to get for her?

You never know what you're going to get with my mother. Sometimes the joke lands and she's right on time with the laugh or the quick response. Sometimes not. And in the realm of Not, many other things can take shape. I have never been able to predict the weather of her moods. This time, she transformed into Joan Crawford, and with an iciness in her voice that could have frozen any pile of Brussels sprouts, she said,

"I have a can of olives. I'll be fine."

And that was how I knew it would be a terrible Christmas.

* * *

I lapsed into my old role on Christmas Day. I made food, I got coffee, I gave big gifts (I had gotten tickets for my whole family to see Prince at Madison Square Garden on December 30th), I kept everything together. Too together. I strung myself out. I probably strung out everyone else, too, but it can be hard to see your own dysfunction in real time.

My mother maintained her Crawford-Esque character throughout the day. The gifts did not impress her (she actually tried to give my brother's girlfriend her ticket to the Prince concert, to punish me), the food was fine, but she did not seem to enjoy the company. I had seen this performance by my mother many times. I knew from experience that it was unchangeable. It was also intolerable.

And then, it snowed.

Snow in Boston can be many things. It can be scenic, it can be fun, and it can be cheerful. It can also be a living hell. Boston got two back-to-back blizzards while were there. It was like *The Shining*, only there was no giant room with a typewriter one might escape to when the mind loss started to set in. No hallway for your tricycle escapades. No hedge maze for some quality time with your personal demons.

Whatever we had hoped this trip might be, it was not. Acceptance of what it was would come years later, after much work, grief, laughter, and time. It would not come while we were there.

I had a show booked during my time in Boston, a sort of homecoming night with members of 33 Slade, Boey's new project, and some other friends. Because Boston laughs at the snow and its proposed limitations, the show still happened. People came out and crammed into a small room in Central Square. Our families, friends, and other folks all showed up. We played our music, we hugged our people, and we did the thing. It was good.

What was not good, was the extended residency of the Crawford performance my mother was now four days into. And now my ex-husband was also in the mix, adding weird energy to what was already a bit much. My mother had not seen my ex since she had helped me pack and move out of the Brooklyn apartment years before. In a healthy family, the reunion might not have been a big deal. I'm not from a healthy family.

For much of my life, my difficulties with other people have resulted in my mother siding with the other person. This has ranged from ex-boyfriends to lapsed friendships, to my brother's father. She has rarely chosen my side in things. It took me a long time to get to a place where I could admit that while my mother probably does love me, she doesn't seem to like me very much.

In the case of my ex-husband on this particular night, it seemed as though she didn't like either of us. I was used to being disliked and punished for existing by her. I was less used to her doing it to anyone else. But toward the end of the show, she decided he would be her chauffeur for the rest of the night. I heard her tell him she needed him to drive her back home. There were other directions in there, too, about stops and things she needed to get. He had driven in from an hour away to be at the show. His parents lived out by Worcester, and that was where he had to drive back to, in the snow. It seemed unnecessary that he should be the one to drive her around Cambridge. I spoke up and offered an alternative, and that was *it*.

I felt the air rearrange itself.

The next day, my fiancé and I left town for New York where we would stay with friends. We reunited with my family members in at Madison Square Garden two days later, for the Prince concert I'd bought us all tickets to see. He was exquisite. He played for two-and-a-half hours. I loved every minute. It was the last time I would ever see him play, but I didn't know it at the time.

My mother, now gunning for a Primetime Emmy nod for Outstanding Lead Actress in a Dramatic Series of Events, did not speak to me at the concert. My brother had talked her out of giving away her ticket, but she made a big show of being there against her will. I'm proud to report that she did not ruin Prince for me, but it was a lot. I vowed to never go back up there for holidays, and I haven't. Some things cost too much, and I'm not talking about money, though the trip was absurdly expensive. As my brother so astutely said of another family trip that wasn't exactly fun:

"We could have gone anywhere."

Gospel.

* * *

I called my mother in mid-January, to talk it out. This was not done in my family. The protocol all of my life had been to fall apart for reasons never named, survive the silence, and then take the call when she decided the freeze was over—sometimes months later. Under no circumstances did anyone ask a question or propose a chat. Hell no.

She did not take my call. She did not call me back. Instead, she sent me a letter via certified mail. It was typed. It was three pages long. It was double-sided.

The Letter, in all of its abusive glory, was an itemized outline of all the things my mother had disliked about me since childhood. I had been right. She didn't like me. Alongside the list of my failures and faults, there was also an undercurrent of "don't tell anyone I did this" woven into the text. She wanted to be able to tell me what was wrong with me in her estimation, and she wanted me to keep it a secret.

I knew something about secrets. I'm a sexual abuse survivor. The first thing people who are violating you say is, "Don't tell anyone." And often, you don't. There are a number of reasons why you don't. They range from fear to not knowing what the alternative is, to even trusting the person, depending on who they are in your life. But for sure, underneath all of that, is shame. It's horrifying to be violated, and it's horrifying to have to say it out loud. The words are gross, ugly, and dark.

A huge part of you believes that there's something about you that caused the abuse in the first place. And then, before you know it, it's lodged in your system as a core belief. Core beliefs are the place from which our other ideas, attitudes, and behaviors develop. If shame is a core belief—and it certainly has been for me all of my life—you are prone to take on more things that make you feel ashamed. It becomes an activated mechanism in your life.

For someone to tell me that I should keep something from other people is a red flag. It signals that the person is somewhere on the spectrum of dangerously unwell to unsafe. Wherever they land on that spectrum is of no interest to me. They are disqualified from having any access to me.

I cried. I threw up. I read it thrice.

And then, in giant red letters, I wrote "CONSIDER THE SOURCE" across the top. I folded it up, and I put it away. It's been in a box for ten years. I have never looked at it again. I will never look at it again.

Sometimes I wonder if its mere existence has a radioactive quality, though; if it has a toxic emission, like Chernobyl. Maybe.

I received The Letter two weeks before *Family Album* was released. The decisions about the cover, the artwork, and the copy were made months before. The album came out, dedicated to my mother, and I didn't hear from one person in my family. Not one. My birthday was the next day. Silence.

I used to forget how bad it was every time and then allow it again. So now I write things down. I keep a record. It helps.

* * *

I wish I could say that I blazed through the release of *Family Album* unscathed, but I'd be lying if I did. I did have a big sparkly album release show here in Nashville, and I did manage to make a video for the opening track, "True Story," but I was limping through it. The worst part was that I'd done some of it to myself.

I'd insisted on making the album process one that involved so many people and so much travel. I'd insisted on trying to polish it all up until it shined. And I'd insisted on centering my family. The project was the end of a lot of things for me, not the least of which, was trying to impress my mother. There is no more futile an act than trying to make someone see you. I have scars to prove it.

Additionally flattening, was the truth that it was my second solo album to be released under emotional distress. *Singer* had a tough release season as well. I left a marriage the week before, and my brother went to prison a month later. I was sleeping on couches, eating too little, carrying too much, and trying too hard. The record that took me fifteen months to make, more money than I've ever spent on anything, and so much labor? She never even got a release show. I was too busy driving to Nashville to find a new place to live, a new life.

Albums are births of a sort. You don't know how they'll impact your life until you do, and then you have to apply as much acceptance as possible to the situation. One of the things I have to accept is that my mother will never in my life congratulate me. She will never celebrate me. I grieve it, but I also accept it. What I will not do, is allow her any more access to me in such seasons of vulnerability. It's when I'm vulnerable that she withholds love and support. So, I don't show her any of it. She has to stay all the way over there, so I can celebrate myself.

* * *

"The courage to change the things I can"

What an order.

* * *

My parents used to be collaborators, of course. Both my mother and biological father are songwriters. Before my birth and for a few years after it, they joined forces in the Coconut Grove art scene that was home to many artists and musicians of their generation. They did not plan to have me, nor did they necessarily want to. I was a byproduct of their time together, but once I was born, the romantic facet of the partnership ended. I stayed with my mother and only saw my father sporadically throughout my childhood. I never lived with him, and I never called him anything other than his first name, which is Randy.

There are only a handful of photos from my childhood that feature all three of us. I have two. Most of the other photos from his visits are of him and my mother, both playing guitar and singing. I just happened to also be there. His disinterest lasted until he casually cut ties with me when I was fifteen. No event of note or argument preceded it. I didn't even know him well enough to argue with him. He had spent most of my childhood being sulky, occasionally lecturing me about his views on rock music and how the only great American rock musician had been Jimi Hendrix. Right before he wandered out of my life for good, he said, "Never forget: the Left Banke did 'Walk Away Renee.'" I haven't forgotten. I've also never found any use for that information.

By the time I was recording *Family Album*, it had been many years since I'd seen or heard from him. I had grown up hearing his songs as well as the ones he'd written and recorded with my mother and another terrific songwriter named Mark Bass. I hoped to include one of his songs on the album, but how? Unlike "Little Bit of Rain" by Fred Neil, which could be licensed, Randy's work was obscure. My mother and brother had contributed songs to the project, but they had given me permission to record them; they're also featured on the recordings. Randy was a horse of a different color.

I'd had a little bit of contact with his one sister, Alice, in my adulthood. She maintained light communication with him. I asked her for his email address, and she obliged. I proceeded to send the strangest email of my life, asking my own father if I could record his song, "Easy Now." He wrote back, giving me permission. He did not ask me about myself, and he did not offer anything about himself. And then, at the bottom of the message, he signed his full name. Like we'd never met. His *full name*.

For years, I tried to convince myself that he had done that for legal purposes—just as I'd tried to justify his absence from my life for so many years. I'd cheer it up for other people with phrases like, "I got the family I was supposed to have," or other crowd-pleasers like, "I might have been protected by his absence." People love when women make the damaging behaviors of others no big deal. We're encouraged to do it—rewarded for it, even.

But it was crushing. It was. I still recorded and released the song, and it does seem to belong on that record of broken dreams, but *Jesus Christ*. What a thing. What a new brand of absence.

I didn't send him the album when it came out, as I once would have. I didn't send it to my mother either. And my brother's father acts as though the record never happened. He liked *Singer*, and that was my last record as far as he's concerned.

But it wasn't the last record. As I've learned the hard way:

Pretending doesn't make a thing untrue; it just makes you unavailable to the truth. There's a difference.

Definition of *voice*

noun

5

distinction of form or a system of inflections of a verb to indicate the relation of the subject of the verb to the action which the verb expresses

Simply Said

This is the last one for a while. We don't know how long yet, but it will be a couple of years, at least. The sentencing is supposed to be in February and right now, everything about it is unknown. They could stack his charges, make him serve them end-to-end, or they could let him serve concurrently. It could be as long as ten years. Unimaginable.

Christmas is in five days. If I sleep between now and then it will be a miracle. His house is full of people, which is part of it. But my mind is full of noise; it has been since the arrest eleven months ago. It's not all about him. My mind has its own noise and I've never known how to adjust the volume. Five days until the last Christmas. Who needs a quiet mind?

* * *

I sobbed through the entire meeting. No one cared. They'd all seen it before—they'd all *done* it before. That's one thing about being in an Al-Anon meeting: you don't have to perform. You don't have to do anything. You can share or not. You can cry or laugh. You can tell the truth. For some people, it's the only place any of that is possible. In the beginning, I was one of those people.

My brother was taken into custody on March 26th. He'd been arrested nearly fifteen months prior. All of the time in between was a season of waiting. I had filled the time. I had made parts of two albums, I had rallied the troops, and I had left myself behind.

I realized that about a month before he went in. I found myself walking a mile in the freezing cold of a Massachusetts February. I was on my way to cancel his video membership so he wouldn't have to pay while he was in prison. I hadn't packed enough warm clothing and was becoming a human popsicle while doing a fool's errand. He didn't need me to do it. No one needed me to do anything, and yet, there I was. Doing.

It was a way to live through the fear. The fear was so great, that I couldn't live with it in my body unless I kept moving. So, I did.

My real life was back in Brooklyn. My cats. My marriage. My career. Two of the three were on very unsure footing. At least cats are always great.

I left Boston after the video store visit. I went home to face the literal and proverbial music. I had an album to release, a marriage to undo, and a life to reclaim. No big deal.

I left my marriage on a Tuesday, celebrated a birthday that Saturday, started Al-Anon the following Monday, and released *Singer* the day after that, on a Tuesday. It was a big week.

I already spoke the language of 12 Step recovery. I'd gone to Alateen as a kid and had sat in hundreds of AA meetings with a recovering elder when I was growing up. By the time I was coming back as an adult, I knew it was exactly where I belonged. So many parts of my life were in flux, the best that I could do was no harm. To me, to them, to anyone.

The pending incarceration had become the main topic in everyone's life, including mine. Even if my thoughts got away from it for a moment, it would jump back into the frame, and waves of grief and fear would wash over me. *It wasn't supposed to be like this*, I thought. *If only he had fucking listened.* My resistance to accepting life on life's terms was as powerful as it had ever been. Periodically, I would collapse under the weight of the truth and my own rigidity. There was nothing between the two states of being.

In the meetings, I was hearing about letting him be, living my life as I saw fit, and doing the next right thing. They all sounded great. Implementing them was a whole other thing.

* * *

Bo and I are an odd set, and yet, a perfect set. We are technically half-siblings. My father is the apathetic songwriter who may or may not know my birthday. His father is the owner of the Brown House. We share a mother, a history, and the language of music. But it goes much deeper than that.

With the exception of the years I spent in Miami with his father, we were raised together. Not only did it not come up that we were half-siblings, but I'm not sure Bo even realized it until we were in our teens. I called his father "Dad." My father was largely absent, and when he did drop by, he didn't treat me like his daughter. All told, I'm betting my brother has seen my biological father fewer than five times in his life. It's like that.

When Bo was sixteen and I was nineteen, I let him move in with me. Our parents had their own things going on and living with either of them would have placed him back in Miami, or up in New Hampshire where our mother was moving. I didn't want him back in Miami. I had been through that and didn't want it for anyone. That house isn't a home. And moving to New Hampshire would have meant another school, another transition. I had also done that. All told, I had attended five high schools in four years.

He would come live with me.

We were like mini adults in that apartment. We rented the top floor of a house in Belmont, Massachusetts, the town where he was attending high school. A two-bedroom with an attic space. It was us, my cat, and his dog. He went to high school every day and I went to work. He worked some nights and weekends at an ice cream shop with a bunch of his friends. It was stable. It was safe.

We eventually grew up and out of that space, but we stayed close to one another. The band continued on for years, we lived together in other spaces, and we were a set. A fact of life. Buick and Boey, period. My identity as a human was inextricably linked to being his sister. The parents had all been so uneven with their love and presence in my life, Bo was the only true constant. And beyond that, we liked each other.

I had friends who modeled remarkably different dynamics with their siblings. My first boyfriend regarded his sisters like they were coworkers of his in an office somewhere. I knew women who hated their brothers. Not me and Bo. Whatever else could be said about us, we liked each other. And when we played music together, we shared a mind. I didn't understand it then, but Bo and I didn't have to verbally work out any of our musical ideas. We just knew. It's rare in this life. I know that now.

* * *

Our band had split by the time he was arrested. I was in San Diego recording a song for *Singer* called "The Streets of My Town" when I got the call. Session over.

Everything over.

The things I had been trying to outrun and outlive had finally caught one of us. And I had to go back and look. What's more, I had to admit that I had been the only one running.

* * *

I spent the month leading up to his incarnation recalibrating my entire life. I worked; I slept in fits and starts on various couches (my ex and I were splitting time at our apartment, but even when I had it, I slept on the couch); and I went to Al-Anon meetings. I went as often as I could, which was sometimes two or three times a day. Meetings were the only places I felt normal, a word I use loosely. I felt like one of many, instead of like a defective misfit—which was how I felt everywhere else. I was grieving too many things at once to be able to parse them out. When you're in that much pain, the regular world can feel flat and unfriendly. One thing New York has going for it, though: you can cry anywhere. New Yorkers keep on moving.

I was starting to have the smallest amount of self-regard, and with that came self-knowledge. One solid truth emerged: I didn't want to be there when they took my brother into custody. I didn't want to see it, to have the memory. I felt like a walking trauma wound as it was. I was afraid that if I saw it with my own eyes, I'd never unsee it. I decided not to go.

This was as radical a decision as I could have made at the time. In truth, it was more radical than leaving my marriage. This was way outside of who I and everyone else had known me to be. But it felt right, and I quietly carried it around as an idea. As the date grew closer, I felt the pull of the old behavior. I found myself calculating driving times between New York and Boston, doing the math to see if I could still get there in time. But I didn't want to. It was nothing more than an old alarm going off.

I told him I wasn't coming, but I didn't tell anyone else. It wasn't anyone else's business. It was mine and his. I was also learning about that.

The night before his date, I could barely speak in my Al-Anon meeting. I sobbed through a share about what was happening, and about how I was trying not to go. The room was full. There were so many of us that rows of seats had been added to the already large circle we were seated in. Everyone listened as I sobbed, and at the end of the meeting, several people came up to me and asked me for my phone number. I happily gave it to them. I needed all the help I could get.

My phone rang every thirty minutes throughout that night, right up until the morning. They had made a phone tree and decided to take turns calling me, to make sure I was still doing what I wanted and not what I felt I was expected to do. They were helping me hold on to myself until it was too late to get there in time to see my brother. They got me through it, and without judgment. A room full of strangers.

The morning was achingly painful. I had indeed made it past any departure time that would have gotten me to the event, but I hadn't made it past the calls from my family and Bo's friends. They were incredulous. Was I really not coming? Was I really that selfish? Was this really how I was going to let this day unfold?

I had just enough recovery to stay away. But not enough to turn my phone off.

I walked around Brooklyn. I cried. I got through it. And then, Bo called. It was ten minutes before he would be taken into custody, ten minutes before his two-and-a-half-year sentence at a Massachusetts state prison would begin. I took the call. I asked if he was okay. He said he was. And then he said:

"I'm so glad you're not here."

I choked, "You are?" Tears streamed down my face; my throat ached with withheld sobs.

He said, "Yeah, can you imagine?"

I was free.

The last things I said to him were to remember who he really was and that I loved him.

He went to prison. I left for Nashville the next day, with his drum kit in my van. We'd be okay.

* * *

If you change one thing, you change everything. The first boundary seemed unimaginable, but then it got easier. I had that first one to lean on, to remember who I was in that moment, and I borrowed courage from it as I went. The day I decided to do what was best for me was the beginning of the life I live now. The first brick. It has also made me a better person to the people I'm in relationships with today, including my brother.

There is a group of people I've never seen again, whose faces have faded with time, and whose names I'd never get right; those people are forever in that story with me. They held the line. If you're one of them and you find these words:

Thank you.

But Now I Do

In the dream, I'm backstage at a theater, about to get on stage and play my solo music. People are telling me I have five minutes until stage time. I'm wearing my guitar, but I don't know my songs. I haven't played them in years and now there's an audience that expects me to deliver. *What capo position was "Brilliant Mistakes"? Was there a capo? E minor for the bridge? What other songs were there? How did they go?*

I would wake up panicked, my left hand making the shapes of guitar chords. And then waves of grief and shame would wash over me. I knew it wasn't just a dream. It was a part of myself calling me back, a part I'd abandoned years before.

I had that dream for years.

* * *

Sixteen drag queens are a tough act to follow. We were in the mostly empty parking lot of a gay bar in Nashville called Trax. A friend of mine had played a minor role in planning the event, a tribute to a deceased-but-legendary drag queen who had also been an AIDS activist. That was how I got involved. The primary organizer had originally asked for my band, Friendship Commanders, to play, but we couldn't do it. Ever the helper, I offered to play my solo music with a full band instead. That was fine with them.

Was it fine with me? What music? The old songs? How would I make them sound like me in this chapter? Who would play with me?

All good questions.

My partner and bandmate said he was in right away. We asked our friend Lex Price to play bass. Lex had played with me in the Before Times, before I put it all away. He's long been my favorite bassist in Nashville. He said he was in, too. Then we asked our friend Kris Donegan, a terrific local guitarist who was down for weird stuff and good causes. I had never played with Donegan before, but I had a feeling about him. He said yes.

I had a handful of unreleased songs from my previous solo chapter that had never been recorded, but which I still loved. They stood out among the hundreds that had been written, demoed, and archived. I dusted them off and threw in a few that had been recorded and released on my first two albums. I think there was one Friendship Commanders song in there, too, for good measure. Great. Rehearse, shape it up, play the show, and put everything back where it lived: in the closet.

To be fair, we thought it would be an event. It wasn't. The organizer had come into some personal issues in the months leading up to the show, and the whole thing had fallen apart. But we were already there, so we would play.

Other acts had shown up, too. There were bands, solo performers, a DJ, and at last: the drag revue.

Whoever put us after them had truly overestimated the power of rock music.

When it was our turn, we loaded our pared-down gear onto the stage. By stage, I mean plywood on a platform that buckled when we moved. The PA system was the one the DJ brought. It was too late to back out. We kept going.

I'm certain no one heard the vocals, but I sang like it was my last performance on earth. We had silently agreed to play as loudly as the gear would allow us to, and the dance music PA was no match for the amps. Maybe ten people watched us, but we played like it mattered. Still, I felt mortified that I had asked some of Nashville's best musicians to come and play for free to nearly no one. But at the end of our set, as we were walking off stage, Kris said, "We should make a record."

I felt something shift in me.

* * *

I released *Family Album* on February 22nd, 2011. I played a release show that month, in Nashville. I made one video, though the people who made it took fourteen months to complete it. By the time it was ready, the record had come and gone, like a tree falling in the woods. I played a handful of solo shows in the years that followed, the last of which was in June of 2013. And then, I put it all away. It wasn't dramatic or grand. It wasn't decisive or declarative. It was quiet. It was private. One day, I wasn't her anymore. *Thank god.*

I had come to hate that woman. I hated her dresses, her songs about love, loss, and family; I hated her messes. There were so many messes, so many questionable behaviors, choices, and projects that filled her back pages. I wanted something else, someone else. I wanted to save myself *from* myself. I started a metal band.

I cataloged all the handmade dresses and hung them in the upper tiers of my one closet; it became a tiny museum of lost personhood, rejected ideas, and failed attempts. I sold the shoes, the mandolin, and the ukulele (*who needs a ukulele?* I thought). I closed up shop. And I left her there. Most of the time, it was fine. Most of the time, *I* was fine.

But sometimes she would call me back in my dreams. And once in a while, during the day, my whole system would ache with grief. There are many things to grieve in this life: other people, death, divorce, disappointment, etc. But grieving part of one's own self has a different gravity to it. It can be arresting.

* * *

After the parking lot show, I thought about what Donegan had said. *He didn't mean it*, I thought. But still. He didn't love me; he didn't have to say kind things. He didn't even really know me. He was simply making a passing statement at a ridiculous moment, but I had been wearing it close to my heart and re-examining it ever since.

A *record*.

I was about to release a record that my band Friendship Commanders had made with Steve Albini called *BILL*. It was a dream project made with a dream collaborator and I had beat my demons in the process of doing it. I had played all the guitars. I had sung the vocals for the thirteen-song album in six hours in front of Albini and Jerry. *To tape.* I had prepared for months in advance, talking with myself about how no one's feedback mattered but my own. I would not collapse into being bullied by anyone, not even Steve fucking Albini. I had promised myself.

For all the talk that had circulated about Steve over the years, you'd almost expect him to be the worst among them. I loved his engineering work and his band Shellac, but I had no idea if he'd be the harsh critic to end all critics. I was willing to go anyway. I'd already lived through the worst of it. He was just a man.

After my first vocal passes, I went upstairs to the control room to listen back, both for sounds and performances. I felt naked, in the spotlight. Steve didn't look up from the board but turned some knobs before the playback started and said:

"Well. Turns out you're a great singer."

I didn't need to hear it, but it was good to hear.

Friendship Commanders didn't start out as a way to prove my former self wrong, but it ended up doing just that. In my back pages, I had grown to believe that I wasn't a real guitar player; in Friendship Commanders, I am the only guitar player. I had grown to believe that I was a pitchy vocalist who had issues with power; in Friendship Commanders, I sing at the absolute top of my vocal capacity, and my pitch is fine. I had been told that my songwriting wasn't rocket science; in Friendship Commanders, I have written the shit out of all kinds of music that crosses genre and stylistic lines. Last, I had once believed I had to work with friends in order to be safe; in Friendship Commanders, I work with professionals, and I've never been so safe. The old beliefs were garbage. I had systematically replaced them all. With brute force.

The idea I kept coming back to after Donegan's passing proposal was, what if I can do this now? What if I can apply what I learned in Friendship Commanders to the solo work? What if I can trust myself?

What if.

There *were* those songs. I had to admit that playing the five unreleased songs had felt great. I'd always wanted to record them, but I hadn't wanted to deal with what came after. Maybe I could just track them with the dudes and release them as an EP, some little thing to mention once on my socials, and then forget about.

I was doing it again. Was I already calling the project *little*? I sounded like my parents. Yuck.

The songs the songs the songs . . . the songs were . . . not who I was anymore. They were so fucking *nice*. She was always trying to soften the blow, to make it pretty. Also, yuck. But if this was going to work, I wasn't allowed to hate her. That had been the problem then, so it wasn't going to be the solution now. Whatever I'd done before, I would do the opposite. Oh, the records used to take a hundred years to complete? I'd make this one in a day. I had hated myself to the core of my being? I would practice radical self-acceptance. I had let inferior men play my guitar parts? I would play on the whole goddamned record. I had hated my voice? I would sing with abandon. I had shared production credit even when I had made all the calls? None of that. One producer this time: me.

That settled it, then.

And as far as the issue of the songs went: yes, they were written in her voice, from her perspective. But they were great songs. So, I'd answer them, in this voice. From here. Tell the truth about what really happened in those stories—that marriage, those collaborations, that family, that . . . me. I would tell the truth about me.

* * *

182

I decided to make the record at Sound Emporium, Studio A. It's a beautiful room here in Nashville with a vibe for days and a client list that's almost unbelievable. But just as important: it has a woman manager. I'd never worked at a studio run by a woman before, and while it wasn't on my list of things to do differently this time, why not cross off one more?

I booked one day. That's it. A local engineer named Justin Francis was hired. And then Jerry, Lex, Kris, and I made a record. We tracked nine of the ten songs in one day as a band. Like regular people. What a thing. I tracked the vocals myself at our home studio between Friendship Commanders tours. And then, for the tenth track, I did a solo performance of a song called "Simply Said." I had written it at my brother's old house during the Christmas season before his incarceration. I called eight female musicians here in town and asked them to join me on the refrain, and they did.

And that was it.

No one told me I was tone deaf, no one told me I wasn't good enough to sing my own songs, and no one took weird shots at my writing or playing. And I didn't either. I was tempted to, but I didn't.

If you change one thing, you change everything.

I had changed *me*.

The most remarkable part of the process was singing the original five songs the way they were written. I invited the spirit of my former self into the room when I sang those tracks; I allowed her to advise and shape my choices. I might have changed, but I was able to sing them one more time for her, the way she had heard them in her head. She deserved that.

There was healing in updating the stories in the new songs, too. I got to say things I had never had the chance to in real life. I got to close the book on things I had regarded as still open. I got to own the narrative. I used to think that because I wasn't a hero, the narrative itself was shameful. But it's not. It's just human.

My relationships didn't all make it. I cut ties with several of the people in the stories years ago. The ones I didn't cut ties with don't have unlimited access to me anymore. And some of them are still in my story, I'm happy to report. Bo and Levi are still very present in my current life. They both do and make cool stuff and I'm grateful to share so much road with them, past and present.

My relationship with myself is the one that really emerged, though. It took me a long time, but I was finally able to circle back for that girl in the eighth grade in the Harley Davidson shirts; that sixteen-year-old who spoke up and paid the price; that young bride who didn't know; and that singer-songwriter who believed in everyone more than she believed in herself. I was able to tell their stories and sing their songs. It had to take as long as it took. If I had done it even a year earlier, I'm not sure I would have been able to see it through. Not with love. I had been able to do it with love for myself. A miracle.

All of this was right on time. I'm so grateful I lived to tell.

Acknowledgments

When I first had the seeds of ideas for this album and essay collection, I did not know that the project would become the behemoth it has. I've been running alongside the work, trying to keep up with it. Now it exists, and I almost can't believe it. I owe many thanks.

To Jerry: thank you for loving me through it, believing I could do this even when I didn't, and listening along the way. And thank you for your many talents, all inspiring. You are my home.

To Lex and Kris: thank you for saying yes, for showing up, for bringing yourselves to the music, and for laughing with me. I am so grateful to have had your support.

To Bo: thank you for the life story, for letting me tell some of yours, and for being happy for me. I'm so happy for you, too. And proud of you.

To Nanc: thank you for always claiming me.

To Levi: thank you for the years of friendship, the music, and the present.

To Julie and Magan: thank you for me helping learn how to show my honest self. There are no words.

To Doug Sax and Arthur Klein: posthumous thanks for seeing me. It saved my life.

To the women who have taught me how to tell my stories by telling theirs, especially Nora: you will never know.

And to you, listener, and reader: many thanks. Without you, it's just me and the truth.

Last, to all of the women and girls I have been: thank you for showing yourselves to me again as I put our experiences down on tape and the page. Thanks for

staying alive through it all, for carrying the narrative.
Feel free to forget it now. We did it.

Thirteen.

About the Author

Photo by Gregg Roth

Buick Audra is a musician, songwriter, and writer living in Nashville, TN. In addition to her solo work, she is also a member of the melodic heavy duo, Friendship Commanders. She has published several essays, but this is her first collection.

www.ingramcontent.com/pod-product-compliance
Lightning Source LLC
Chambersburg PA
CBHW031131090426
42738CB00008B/1046